To my friends at Red Rock!
Here's to education!

Helen Masters

Jefferson County

A Contemporary Portrait

A publication of

The Coalition of Jefferson County
Chambers of Commerce &
Jefferson Economic Council

Helen Masterson

Historical Publishing Network
A division of Lammert Publications, Inc.
San Antonio, Texas

ISBN: 1-893619-00-1

Library of Congress Catalog Card Number: 99-71570

Jefferson County: A Contemporary Portrait

author:	Helen Masterson
photographers:	Susie Masterson
	Bob Scott
contributing writer for *"Partners in Jefferson County":*	Julie Thenell

HISTORICAL PUBLISHING NETWORK

publisher:	Ron Lammert
vice president, marketing:	Barry Black
vice president, operations:	Charles A. Newton, III
project manager:	Wynn Buck
graphic production:	Colin Hart, Debbie Swisher
administration:	Donna Mata, Dee Steidle

The Coalition of Jefferson County Chambers of Commerce

Jefferson Economic Council

The Conifer Chamber of Commerce
P.O. Box 127
Conifer, CO 80433
(303) 838-0178

**The Evergreen Area
Chamber of Commerce**
P.O. Box 97
Evergreen, CO 80437
(303) 674-3412

**The Greater Golden
Chamber of Commerce**
1010 Washington Ave.
Golden, CO 80419
(303) 279-3113

The Jefferson Economic Council
1536 Cole Blvd., Ste. 100
Golden, CO 80401
(303) 202-2965

The Northwest Metro Chamber
Serving Arvada, Westminster &
Northern Jefferson County
7305 Grandview Ave.
Arvada, CO 80002
(303) 424-0313

The West Chamber
Serving Jefferson County
P.O. Box 280748
Lakewood, CO 80228
(303) 233-5555

CONTENTS

Introduction

The land—what it was, what it would produce, and what it would support—tells the story of Jefferson County.

The history of the land can be best seen in "the cut" of the shale hogback sliced to make way for Interstate 70, the main link with the mountains. "The cut" reveals the various changes that occurred during the expanse of time and the forces that uplifted the Rocky Mountains approximately 70 million years ago. Here stratum after stratum is exposed, showing the panorama of progress: earthquakes that changed the position of sea and land; volcanoes that added layers of molten rock; the shallow inland sea that began the creation of the vast plain. On the other side of the hogback, called Dinosaur Ridge, the building of a road, Alameda Parkway, revealed that 50 million years ago dinosaurs roamed this area. The large Jurassic plant-eating dinosaurs wading in the mud left footprints that later transformed into rock. Today on Dinosaur Ridge can be found fossilized dinosaur bones and more than 300 dinosaur footprints.

The human history of the area dates back at least twelve thousand years to when Paleo-Indians, armed with spears, hunted woolly mammoths. When these giant animals became extinct, Indians hunted buffalo, deer, and smaller animals, such as jackrabbits, and gathered wild plants, a lifestyle that existed into the1800s.

Children delight in seeing the real tracks, fossilized bones, or other traces of the creatures that roamed the Hogback, where some 360 dinosaur tracks have been identified.

In 1803, land in Colorado was worth about four cents an acre. That was the bargain price paid by President Thomas Jefferson, who had an eager interest in expanding to the west, to Napoleon for all the territory owned by France west of the Mississippi River. Although the Louisiana Purchase brought the land into the United States, what is now Jefferson County was still Indian country, home of the Arapaho and the Utes. This was territory where these two tribes traditionally hunted—and often clashed with each other—but it was not what they considered their home. None of the Indians offered strong resistance when settlements sprung up in what they regarded as marginal land.

Throughout the fifty years following the Louisiana Purchase, what happened in the rest of the United States had little effect on this part of the west. The opening of the Santa Fe Trail brought fur trappers, traders, and "mountain men" to Colorado, but the decline of the fur trade in the 1830s (beaver hats were no longer in fashion) saw few settlers making their way to what was called the Great American Desert. In 1854, the United States Congress created the Territory of Kansas, which included what is now Kansas, Nebraska, Utah, New Mexico, and Colorado.

It made little difference. Near the foothills of the Colorado mountains, economic growth was slow. But the land, as always, would change Colorado's—and Jefferson County's—history.

The Fort Restaurant in Morrison is a replica of Bents Fort, an 1830s Colorado fur trade fort along the Santa Fe Trail.

Logging, 1920—Trees growing
along the streams became part
of the county's logging industry.
The trees in this picture were
transported into Denver to be
made into bushel baskets.

A Solid Foundation

It was the lure of gold. Nothing else would have drawn settlers into the region in such great masses.

Before 1858, Colorado was for loners. It was a land for those who wanted open spaces and a nomadic life. The plains were dry and barren in the summer, windblown in the winter. The Rocky Mountains loomed as a foreboding barrier for those who had ventured westward. Then came the gold.

The financial panic of 1857 brought economic disaster to many people in the United States. By 1858, many were unemployed with neither money, credit, nor the opportunity to earn a living. As financial problems spread across the country, the East Coast newspapers were full of stories from the

West and the "Pike's Peak Gold Region." The stories of "easily acquired riches" led people all over the country to rush to the Rockies. To them, the American Frontier was a symbol of wealth and opportunity. It was the story of hope and a new beginning, a story often repeated across the entire West. The gold rush started in 1850—in Jefferson County.

That year, gold was discovered by Lewis Ralston near the western edge of what is now Arvada. Although many people washed flecks from the sands of Clear Creek, few made big strikes. In early 1859, however, a rich lode of gold was discovered in the mountains where Chicago Creek joins Clear Creek near Idaho Springs. The rush to find gold in the mountains was on.

Many gold-seekers moved up Clear Creek and beyond. Some were discouraged and went

Downtown Golden, 1870. Washington Street and 12th in downtown Golden. On the right is the Avenue Hotel, on the left, the brick building was where the first Legislature held meetings when Golden was Capitol of Colorado, 1862-1867. Golden is now the county seat of Jefferson County.

back home. Others who didn't find gold moved back to the plains and set up supply stores. Like any resourceful business person, many of these pioneers who came to Jefferson County in 1859 soon realized that a good living could be made by providing supplies to those who were still coming and still seeking the gold.

The discouraged miners, recognizing the agricultural possibilities of the region, turned to farming. These pioneer farmers, most of whom came from farming backgrounds in the east, settled first upon the choice bottom lands along the various streams. The high yield per acre and the ready market found in the mining towns of the nearby

mountains made farming a very profitable enterprise.

Of note is that, in the end, the gold-seekers-turned farmers got their gold. Many farmers were paid with "pinches" of gold dust, the amount held between the thumb and index finger. In the 1860s, a pinch of gold dust was worth twenty-five cents. An egg cost four pinches of gold dust, or $1, a sack of potatoes cost fifteen dollars, or 60 pinches of gold dust.

Unlike gold, agriculture caused no land rush, only modest activity. Many early Colorado farmers were moving from Kansas, Nebraska, or Missouri— part of the westward movement caused by the Homestead Act of 1862. Under the act any man or woman could acquire a 160-acre

Opposite: While the 21st century will see the economy centered on aerospace, computer software, biotechnology and other high technology areas, the historic reliance on farming will remain.

Below: The murals on the side of Foss Drug, the oldest business on Washington Avenue in Golden, show the highlights of that town's history.

farm "for the purpose of actual settlement and cultivation." The applicant for a land grant did not even have to be a citizen of the United States. He or she merely had to declare an intent to become a citizen. The act had a great impact in Europe, where generations of Europeans had never owned land. They flocked to the United States by the shipload, later to move west. When the Civil War ended, homesteaders poured westward. Farmers, usually with their families, settled into open spaces along the Front Range wherever there was water or wherever water could be run in a ditch and onto a field.

Despite an appearance of greenness along the river banks,

Opposite: Belmar was a French-style mansion built by May Bonfils Stanton, daughter of a co-founder of the Denver Post. She used more than one million dollars of a ten million dollar inheritance to build it. On her death, she left her mansion to the Roman Catholic Church, but, as the church lacked funds to maintain the estate, it was destroyed, according to the will, in 1970. Office buildings and a historical park now occupy the grounds.

Above: Tropical plants provide nectar and shelter for the more than 1,200 spectacular butterflies living in the tropical forest of the Butterfly Pavilion.

water is scarce throughout the entire area. In the semi-arid climate, with its light rainfall, access to water determines everything: the amount of crops grown, the number of animals raised, and the growth of towns. Irrigation ditches were essential. Without water brought from streams, nothing would grow.

The first irrigation ditch to make use of Clear Creek water was made with a team of oxen bringing water to the valley around Arvada. Many other ditches were

excavated over the next 10 years, resulting in large agricultural yields. Oats, barley, and wheat were major crops, but crop varieties ranged from corn to cherries, apples to tomatoes. Celery, pumpkins, onion, even melons were grown successfully. To these former gold miners, their wealth now lay in cultivating the land.

While the prairie soil was fertile and with water produced many varieties of crops, the region was still dry and barren. Except for a few cottonwood trees offering shade along the banks of streams, no trees grew on the prairie. Many early settlers, missing the vegetation of the east, sent back home not only for seeds for farming, but seeds to plant flowers and trees. Soon the fields of grain were surrounded by blooming flowers. To these pioneers, Jefferson County is indebted for what is now a landscape full of trees and greenery.

Coloradans are active,
outdoor types with a fondness
for wide-open spaces.

A Mix That Works

A land of contrasts, Jefferson County offers topography ranging from stark to spectacular. Over it all, some of Colorado's highest snowcapped peaks stand as sentinels on the western skyline.

In all, Jeffco sits like a giant irregular triangle on the western edge of metropolitan Denver. Twenty miles wide at the northern boundary, the county stretches from the west 54 miles to its southern-most boundary. With 777 square miles to fill, it is the state's most populous county.

The varied landscape includes flat plains to rolling foothills with both urban and suburban areas. The altitude varies from 5,300 feet in the eastern part to nearly 10,000 feet in the west.

The varied landscape of Jefferson County includes cultivated fields and commercial areas with snowcapped peaks in the background.

The mineral and agricultural resources combine to make for distinct economies within the county. In 1869, large coal seams were discovered on Coal Creek, ensuring fuel supplies for the numerous industries that were beginning to appear in Golden. The valley along Clear Creek from Golden to Denver became one of the finest truck gardening areas in Colorado, celery becoming one of the leading crops. On the plains, cattle followed the buffalo in grazing on the grasses, turning the vast prairie into ranch lands.

In November of 1859, wanting their own self-government, pioneers established the Jefferson Territory, a tract of land comprising all of present-day Colorado with strips of what is now Utah and Wyoming. Jefferson Territory was replaced by

the creation of Colorado Territory, signed into existence by President Lincoln on February 28, 1861. Like the land, the communities are a blend of the old and the new, the large and the small.

Only a few towns were incorporated in the beginning, although many town sites were surveyed and platted. Some failed to survive, such as Rocky Mountain City, which was laid in 1859. The "city" was planned so that the road to Central City would pass through its center. It had a grocery store in a tent and a few settlers, but hopes of a large trading post never materialized. Rocky Mountain City didn't grow and became a ghost town in just one short year.

On the other hand, the historic town of Golden, established in 1859 by George West and named for mine-equipment entrepreneur, Thomas Golden, was strategically located at the mouth of Clear Creek Canyon. It

became a major commercial
center for the western mountain
mining towns and throughout its
early years could boast of two
large flour mills, a paper mill, coal
mines, and a brewery that
furnished a market for the grain
grown in the region—as well as
refreshment for the thirsty.

Golden was the chief center of
enterprise in the region, but it
began at the same time as an
aggressive settlement on the
point where the Platte River and
the Cherry Creek converge. Here
suppliers and servicers stopped
their wagons and put up their
cabins, so that they could supply
and service miners whatever
direction they would go in
seeking gold. Both towns were
growing, competitive, proud and
extremely jealous. That settlement
at the confluence of the Platte
River and Cherry Creek became
Denver, and a rivalry developed
that would last for years between
the two supply towns.

As the first territorial capital of
Colorado (1862-67), the Legislature

Jefferson County and the cities of Lakewood and Wheat Ridge shared the cost of purchasing and developing Crown Hill as a park in 1979.

held its first sessions in Golden. In 1867, Golden and Denver became engaged in a battle over which would become the capital city. Golden lost by one vote. Rumor has it that the vote was bought and that Denver acquired the status of capital through "bribery and skullduggery." These allegations, however, were never proven. Now the county seat, Golden retains its Victorian flavor and its main street has preserved an early western charm.

Wheat Ridge began as a successful wheat growing area as early as 1862. A ridge in the wheat fields extended from Denver to a gathering point for prospectors near 44th and McIntyre known as Arapaho City. When travelers on the Overland Trail spoke of "going out through the wheat ridges," the area was named. As large acreages were sold off for smaller tracts, wheat disappeared and farmers turned to growing apples, strawberries and raspberries.

Numerous nurseries were started, featuring fruit trees, plants, and ornamental shrubbery. In the 1880s, W.W. Wilmore opened his famous Dahlia Nursery and became a national figure in the field. Now a city of quiet neighborhoods, Wheat Ridge is still home to greenhouses and flower producers, and Farmer's Markets still feature products from the area's farms.

Arvada was the first to build an irrigation ditch, making use of Clear Creek water for farming. By 1870 Arvada's bonded debt was $80,000, all incurred in the development of its water system. With water, the agricultural area flourished. Celery, tomatoes, peas, and berries had great success. During the 1860s, by-products of fruit farms such as cider and cider vinegar, found a ready market. Dairies offered butter and

cream. As a rural station on the Colorado & Southern Railroad, Arvada became a major cream shipping point.

Although it was one of the first districts organized by county commissioners when the area became a territory, Lakewood, an agricultural and residential community, was not incorporated until 1969. In that June election, the area was named Jefferson City, but, in the following November election,

Built in 1925, the Arvada Flour Mill, restored by the Arvada Historical Society, provides a glimpse into the past.

voters changed the name to Lakewood, the original name for the community in unincorporated Jefferson County. The threat of annexation into the City and County of Denver (which was annexing unincorporated areas on all sides of the capital city) was the main reason residents voted for incorporation. Remaining agricultural in nature—allowing large gardens, farm animals and especially horses and horse corrals on their property—was

what residents wanted. After much debate, the area was finally incorporated into what is now the county's largest—and most urban—city.

(At that same time, 1969, Wheat Ridge became incorporated, not

As large acreages of farmland were sold off for smaller tracts, numerous nurseries were started featuring fruit trees, plants and flowers.

because of threat of annexation by Denver, but because the residents of Wheat Ridge did not want to be annexed by Lakewood, whose residents they considered to be much too liberal!)

While Lakewood is now the largest community in the county, Jeffco's smallest municipality is Lakeside, home to only one business—Lakeside Amusement Park. The park opened to the public in 1908 and was first called "White City," because of its many white buildings. Lakeside has no city government, and the population is recorded as 11.

Broomfield, located in the northern part of Jefferson County, was once a stop on the famous Pony Express route and a station for the narrow-gauge Denver and Salt Lake Railway. The name for the area came from railroad officials who named it for a local crop, broom corn, that grew beside the railroad tracks.

Westminster became a thriving agricultural community, growing vegetables, grains, and, most notably, apples, which were shipped all over the country. The apple orchards were so vast that in the late 1890s and early 1900s, people from the entire area would come in the spring to enjoy the apple trees in blossom and return in the fall to purchase the fruit. The building of the Denver Boulder Turnpike cut the vast apple orchards in half, but many homes in the area still have apple trees in their yard.

The Bear Creek area retained its rural flavor into the 20th century. As late as 1955, Wadsworth south of Hampden was not paved and farm areas were large. Numerous dairy cow and beef cattle operations were important segments of Bear Creek's economy as late as the 1950s. Rooney Ranch, homesteaded in the 1860s by the Rooneys and located between the Bear Creek area and Morrison, is the oldest ranch in Colorado continuously operated by the same family.

While the prairie communities of Jeffco all have a similar background, the history of the

Numerous roadside stands and farmers markets open in early fall.

mountain communities is varied. Nestled in the foothill's entrance to Bear Creek and Turkey Creek Canyon and Red Rocks Park, Morrison also found its future in the soil, but soil of a different kind. George Morrison, a Quebec stonemason, saw specimens of gypsum founded by prospectors and headed up Bear Creek where, he found gypsum and limestone deposits of unusually fine quality. He built a mill for grinding the gypsum and limestone, hauling the powder to Denver by ox-teams. In later years, Governor Evans of Colorado founded the Morrison Stone, Lime & Town Company and started the South Park narrow-gauge, the first railroad built out of Denver. The line was run to Morrison with plans to build on to South Park, but the route was changed to Leadville and Morrison became only a branch.

Governor Evans, noting that the trip over the branch line offered views of spectacular scenery, built a hotel using the

Morrison white and red sandstone in its construction. The hotel and its location brought visitors and families from Denver to spend the summer months. By 1881, the bustling town of Morrison became home to the Colorado Manufacturing Company, which acquired rights to the property of the Stone, Lime and Town Company and opened and operated some of the finest quarries in the state. In 1876, at a Centennial celebration, the red sandstone mined in Morrison was lauded as "the best sandstone for building purposes in the United States."

It was not the soil or minerals that created a livelihood for the pioneers of Evergreen. Timber was in demand for building sluice boxes and mine shafts, providing lumber for homes on the prairie and, as the West grew,

satisfying the demand for railroad ties. The summer heat on the plains also boosted the Evergreen area. For those who could get away to the mountains, Evergreen became,

Summertime finds community festivals and parades.

Lakeside amusement park is a popular summer attraction.

Evergreen has become a retreat of another kind—a beautiful residential area meeting the growing needs of the county.

The economic growth of Jefferson County is perhaps best illustrated by the area around Waterton. Established in the early 1870s when the South Park Branch of the Colorado & Southern Railway laid rails to Leadville, Waterton was a shipping point for farm produce and fire clay and consisted of a railroad station and water tower. After the railway abandoned the branch, it was best known for the point where vital water resources were diverted to Denver. Today, it is still a crossroads of sorts. It is home to Lockheed Martin, where scientists and technicians work on missions going to Mars.

early in its history, one of Colorado's favorite summer vacation retreats. Today

During the last half of the 19th
Century, trains were the ultimate in
transportation and industries, such
as the Golden Smelter, flourished.

OPEN FOR BUSINESS

Economics — *the study of people in the ordinary business of life*

When people come together, they eventually form into a community, and, as such, they must cope with the universal economic problem: how to make a living. Given natural resources, succeeding in business means deciding what commodities should be produced, how these goods should be made, and for whom they should be produced. In all of this, scarcity is a key fact of economic life.

In Colorado, people came for gold; it was scarce, and they turned to supplying those who were seeking the gold.

The lure of panning for gold and silver from the streams led to the bigger business of mining which created the opportunities for trading companies. This

Contrary to popular belief, metro Denver and most of Jefferson County sit on the plains where man-make lakes are vital to the economy.

Colorado's important railroad heritage is preserved at the Colorado Railroad Museum where more than sixty locomotives and cars are on view.

in turn, produced the blueprint for the commercial development in the next century. The wealth that flowed from the mines was only part of the pattern of growth for the county. The richness in other natural resources helped form a healthy economy.

While smelters were erected for the reduction of ores, manufacturing began to meet the demands of both mining and farming activities. Agriculture expanded with the construction of irrigation systems. Irrigation brought water and agricultural

development to the arid, but fertile plains. With the need for irrigation came the rule-of-thumb arrangement that is still the rule of the west: The first farmer to use the waters of a given stream for irrigation purposes would have a "priority right" over all others. This rule is the foundation of the "water rights" rules in existence today.

While the driving force of business was no longer an offshoot of gold fever, the entrepreneurial spirit born of the gold boom continued to help business grow .

During the first 10 years after the discovery of gold, nevertheless, development was slow. The Civil War claimed citizens for soldiers. Travel across the vast land was difficult. The lifeline that sustained the area was the railroads.

W.A.H. Loveland, the father of the Colorado Central System of Railways, built, with his chief engineer Captain Berthoud, lines from Golden to Cheyenne, Denver, Black Hawk, Central City, and Georgetown. The narrow gauge trains carried out shipments from the mining camps through Clear Creek's narrow canyon to Golden.

Realizing that no town could exist without a rail line to bring in the population and to take out products, businessmen from Denver built their own railroad to Cheyenne, a main stop on the Transcontinental Railroad. After that, Coloradoans built railroad lines across the state in every direction. An Arvada-Denver link of the Colorado Central rail line connected with the Denver-Pacific Railroad and helped move farm produce to new markets across the country. The Denver Northwestern Railway Company, an electric interurban line, served Arvada and Golden and many stops between them.

With the railroads, the livestock industry thrived. Cattlemen drove their herds north from Texas to be fattened on the Colorado and Wyoming grasslands, shipping them later by rail to markets in the East.

The railroads also brought more and more newcomers to Colorado. Some came, as before, to seek a new beginning; others came to admire the scenery. Thousands with asthma or tuberculosis came following doctor's orders.

Although the tuberculosis bacillus had been isolated, tuberculosis was

Victorian charm is found in a Golden Bed and Breakfast.

AMC Cancer Research Center is the nation's first research center to focus exclusively on cancer prevention and control.

rampant at the turn of the century. Treatment was commonly believed to be residence in a high, dry climate. In 1905, the congregation of St. John's Lutheran Church in Denver founded the Evangelical Lutheran Sanitarium Association and built a sanitarium in Wheat Ridge. (The first sanitarium was 15 tent-houses —tents built so fresh air could flow through the buildings year-round.) When the need for a tuberculosis sanitarium decreased, the property and funds were transferred to Lutheran Hospital, what is now Exempla Lutheran Medical Center, a major medical facility. The Jewish Consumptives' Relief Society was started in Lakewood to serve those with tuberculosis and other respiratory diseases. Today, JCRS is the site of the AMC Cancer Research Center devoted to the prevention of cancer and chronic diseases.

For twenty-five years before World War II, however, all was quiet in Jefferson County. Growth stopped, even declined. Mining had suffered with the fluctuation in price for both gold and silver. World War I had changed the food habits of Americans who had gone "wheatless" and "meatless" to help the war effort and who then continued to consume less wheat and meat. American population growth was slowing down while better machinery and better methods increased the yield per acre for the production of more human food—food for a market that did not exist. Mechanized farming together with the use of trucks and automobiles cut down the demand for crops such as hay and oats for horses.

Tourists still came, but mainly to see the Rocky Mountains from railroad coaches or, after the

introduction of the automobile, to drive through the area to the rugged mountains. Little of this contributed to the commerce of Jefferson County.

The twenties saw a growth in industrialism that lead to the growth of the cities, but that growth was confined to specific industries, mostly in other portions of the country. Little of this industrial growth contributed to the commerce of Jefferson County.

Even the Depression had little impact on the area. Many residents left farming to work in the growing town of Denver while living quietly in the county. Money was not plentiful, but most residents, drawing on their farming background, lived on large enough plots of land to allow them to raise chickens and a few milk cows and have a garden to provide vegetables.

It would appear that the glory years had passed. No "gold" of any kind appeared on the horizon.

The Jefferson County Courts and Administration Building, nestled in the foothills, is nicknamed the Taj Mahal because of its design and trademark glass dome that towers above an atrium floor.

OPEN FOR BUSINESS—AGAIN

World War II changed everything. Just as surely as the gold rush brought dramatic changes to the Western frontier, events directly related to the war shaped the future of the Front Range.

During the war, farmers were encouraged to expand operations to meet the demand for food. Existing factories were converted to build war-time products while an array of new businesses was created to fulfill the demand for various services.

But it was the location of Colorado that caused startling economic changes. With the war, in-land Colorado became home to military training camps and federal facilities that brought thousands of servicemen and wartime transfers to the area. For example, the

Jefferson County is a major population and employment center with an economy transformed from one based on farming, ranching and natural resource development to one based on services and retail trade.

Above: The Denver Federal Center, a former munitions plant, is now home to numerous federal government agencies.

Right: Colorado School of Mines, the oldest educational institution of higher learning in Colorado, has a national reputation for being one of the finest schools of its type in the country.

Remington Company operated an arms factory at what is now the Denver Federal Center, home to various federal agencies. Many servicemen and federal employees returned after the war to make their home on the Front Range.

Even with the end of the war, federal programs continued to contribute to the economy and federal employment grew steadily. The combination of federal programs and agencies created a base of highly educated workers. This in turn, brought a higher standard of living which resulted in the urbanization of Jefferson County. In all, the "youthful" attitude and active lifestyle prevalent today can be traced to the young, well-educated people entering the job ranks in the late 1940s and early 1950s.

The state's universities also "went to war." Colorado School of Mines trained engineers; the University of Colorado had a language school for the Navy; Denver University trained air corps personnel; Colorado State University housed quartermaster units. At the end of the war, many veterans returned to the state. They, along with returning native-Coloradoans, took advantage of the GI Bill to return to college, to receive vocational rehabilitation training, to use home loan

The outcroppings of rocks provide an almost lunar setting for a home.

Right: In the information age, business locations are coming to Jefferson County because of the superior quality of life and the brain power and skill levels of its population.

Below: Evergreen, a mountain community on the banks of Bear Creek,is surrounded by mountains covered with pine and spruce trees. A dam across Bear Creek created an artificial lake for boating in the summer and ice skating in the winter.

benefits, or to receive business loans. The impact of the war and the benefits accorded to veterans following the war brought distinct changes to the area, and Jefferson County jumped from an economy based on farming, ranching, and natural resource development to one based on manufacturing, retail trade, and services—skipping altogether the heavy industrial phase typical of the traditional economic cycle of other parts of the country. Jefferson County was now becoming a major employment and population center. Even the quiet mountain communities felt the impact of the migration of people to the state. Evergreen moved from a summer retreat to a commuter town of mostly year-round residents.

The rapid acceleration in research devoted to military

needs brought wartime transfers to the state for scientific reasons. Once the war ended, both private and public research continued to expand utilizing the scientific base left at war's end.

Martin Marietta Company (now Lockheed Martin Astronautics) came to Colorado

Lockheed Martin Astronautics has built portions of Martian missions since Mariner 9 orbited and took pictures in 1971. The Mars Pathfinder explored Mars with a Lockheed camera after landing in a Lockheed aeroshell.

in 1955 and located near Waterton. Over the years, the Astronautics contractor has built portions of missions to Mars: the orbit of Mariner 9, the probe of the surface by Viking I and II, and the Mars Pathfinder, which explored Mars with a Lockheed

camera after landing in a Lockheed aeroshell.

From 1952 until 1989, Rocky Flats, located on the northern border of Jefferson County, employed 25,000 workers and produced plutonium triggers for atomic weapons. In 1989, almost all of the site's production of radioactive material was suspended due to safety and environmental concerns related

Commercial firms such as Johns Manville have gone to great lengths to preserve the natural setting while maintaining high-quality work environments.

economy, a series of scientific-research-operations have found a home and tremendous opportunities in Jefferson County.

Still a supply point, the county is home to digital nerve centers, data management, and software development. Manufacturing has grown as companies recognize the advantages of a location in the west with easy access to national markets. The central location has become advantageous for firms with national and/or international operations. Aerospace, financial services, computer software, telecommunications, and biotechnology all draw upon the highly educated work force, a source of scientific and technical personnel, and, of course, the element of Colorado living.

to site operations. In 1992, with the cancellation of the W-88 Trident Warhead, nuclear weapons production at Rocky Flats came to a permanent end. Now the 6,450 acre Rocky Flats Environmental Technology Site is moving toward safe cleanup and reuse.

Since the oil and gas-induced slowdown in the mid-80s followed by a recession in 1987, businesses on the Front Range have worked hard to build a diverse economy. Through the efforts of leaders to attract new industries and balance the

Recreational activities such as Little League are important to families in Jefferson County.

PEOPLE IN THE ORDINARY BUSINESS OF LIFE

Throughout the years, many distinctive people have passed over this treeless, barren ground. Little Raven (Chief Hosa) was born in the early 1800s as the Arapaho began migrating into the area. As a boy he climbed the hill where the lone hackberry tree grew to look for buffalo and watch for Ute war parties. As a chief, he and his Arapahos often camped with the early settlers. Colorow, a Ute Chief, with members of his tribe, was a frequent visitor to what is now Jefferson County. Colorow Point on Lookout Mountain is named after him.

The story of Jefferson County, however, is the story of many people. Although the pioneers of Jefferson County were gold seekers, the history of Jefferson County is also a history of "go backs"—people who

Dinosaur Ridge on West Alameda Parkway just west of C-470 contains both footprints and fossil remains of creatures that roamed Jefferson County 100-150 million years ago. Free, self-guided walking tours follow a mile-long route along the shoulder of the paved road over the Hogback.

So it was with Iron Springs Ranch, better know as Rooney Ranch, at the foot of Dinosaur Ridge. Alexander Rooney came west looking for gold. Finding little, he returned to Ohio. Leaving the gold fields of Colorado, he saw in the valley east of the Hogback a green mountainside with an abundance of water. A year later, in 1860, he returned with his bride and staked claim to the area known as Iron Springs for the medicinal springs used by the Indians. At one time through homesteading and land grants, the family owned 4,480 acres of land—land with grassland for raising cattle and horses and land rich in coal and clay. The stone barn built in 1860 still stands near the stone house completed in 1865. Named to the National Register of Historic

Above: A series of three-toed imprints left about 100 million years ago by dinosaurs can be seen today on Dinosaur Ridge.

Below: The Hogback Geological Exhibit on Interstate 70, known as "The Cut," is a geological cross-section site with a walk way along the rock face.

came to the gold fields of Colorado only to go back to their family homes. But, as has been true throughout the state's history, those who came to Colorado and left, often returned to stay.

Places, the ranch has been home to five generations of Rooneys.

On the north side of the county, the story of Church Ranch tells the typical western story of enterprise and perseverance. George Henry Church arrived in Colorado by ox train in 1859. Like others, he went into the mountains investing in mining claims. When this proved unprofitable, he went back to Iowa. Returning to Colorado on his honeymoon, he made a home first at the mouth of Mount Vernon Canyon, moving south of Broomfield on Old Wadsworth in 1864. Here Church established the first stage stop north of Denver on the road to Cheyenne. Like other pioneers, Church realized that water was necessary to make the land productive. He built a ditch from the mouth of

Coal Creek Canyon to provide water for the first irrigation reservoir in the state. To provide additional water, a tunnel was built by hand under Berthoud Pass to bring water from the west side of the Pass. Thus began the first of many trans-continental

Above: The first overnight stop on the Overland Stagecoach route from Denver was Church's Crossing on Walnut Creek between Broomfield and Westminster.

Below: The pedestrian-friendly Westminster Promenade is connected through trails and walkways with the Westminster City Park and the Butterfly Pavilion.

diversion water systems now so much a part of the state's water system. Church also brought the first Hereford cattle to the area and planted successfully the first wheat in the state.

W. A. H. Loveland, who emigrated to California, moved back to Illinois and crossed the plains in 1859 with his family and an ox train loaded with merchandise, stopped finally in Golden and soon became one of the most successful merchants in the West. Loveland was a politician who, while trying to build the town of Golden, was frequently in sharp conflict with the builders of Denver. As the originator of the Colorado Central System of Railways, Loveland was known as an empire builder who started the railroad history of Colorado.

Another prominent Coloradoan, Adolph Herman Joseph Coors, an industrious, farsighted emigrant is also a part of Colorado's legacy. Born in Barmen, Prussia in 1847, Adolph Coors came to America in 1869 to work at a brewery in

Naperville, Illinois. Pursuing his dream of starting his own brewery, he moved to Denver, where he worked as a gardener and purchased a partnership in the bottling company of John Straderman. By the end of 1872, Coors was sole owner of the business. Although his bottling business was successful, Coors' ambition as a brewer was still his dream. He purchased a half interest in a brewery operated by Jacob Schueler in Golden. With his grim determination to succeed, Coors owned the brewery within three years. He moved it to an abandoned tannery on the eastern edge of Golden at the mouth of Clear Creek Canyon. In 1914, when Colorado voters elected to become a dry state, Adolph Coors, with the help of his three sons, converted the plant to manufacturing malted milk. The

scientific purposes. Today, Coors is America's third largest and the world's ninth largest brewer.

Of course, who could forget the showman: Buffalo Bill Cody, the Pony Express rider who wanted fame and fortune; or the saint: Mother Cabrini, the first American saint, who spent years ministering to the needs of Colorado's poor. It is told that after she founded an orphanage in Denver, she purchased 900 acres in Mt. Vernon for a summer home for

porcelain business started by Coors in 1903 also flourished during Prohibition, producing a variety of products such as cookware, dinnerware and chemical porcelain used for

the children. The mountains were bare without streams and the rainfall was inadequate. She asked the nuns to move a nearby large rock and up came bubbling water. Her dreams for a summerhouse for the children from the orphanage were fulfilled. The little spring still bubbles, furnishing water for the Cabrini Shrine. The statue of Mother Frances Xavier Cabrini can be seen today overlooking I-70.

These are the people who built Jefferson County—coming west prepared to start from the ground up. People like Benjamin Wadsworth, who took a squatter's claim on a piece of land and had it surveyed. Today, all of Arvada east of Wadsworth is now situated on it; Martin and Michael Leyden, who discovered coal by accident and built an enduring industry; Louis Klumker and William Groebels, who built a tannery in 1888 south of Arvada employing skilled workers who had learned their trade in their native Germany; Sara E. Robbins and

her husband, who started the Robbins Incubator Company in a small dugout at the now busy corner of West Colfax and Kipling.

These are also the people who helped mold the Jefferson County character—along with the farmers and ranchers who helped stabilize the county, the young mothers who came west over the treeless plains with their children and helped the communities prosper, the emigrants who left Europe to escape the oppression of wars and who gave the region a strength that has carried it through good times and bad— and, definitely, the families who sent back East for seeds to plant flower gardens.

Then, as now, people came because they thought they might get ahead, put some space between them and the next person, and call it home. People stayed because they found it beautiful, healthy, exciting and different.

Many areas still have a small town feel where children have room to play in the fall leaves.

QUALITY OF LIFE—COLORADO'S GREATEST ASSET

For years, a major Colorado daily carried this saying on the front page: "'Tis a privilege to live in Colorado." In the optimistic-but-still-uncertain 50s, the state's slogan was: "Smile! You live in Colorado." Today, ask anyone why they live in Colorado and the answer is three words: Quality of Life.

What is quality of life? It's knowing a hot summer day will always turn into a cool summer night, or the snowstorm of today will yield to sunshine tomorrow. It is sunsets and unending landscapes like waves of the sea. It's majestic mountain views that represent strength and assurance. It's dry, invigorating air. It is the fresh breeze through the bedroom window at

Occasional visitors to a backyard.

People—and deer—think
Colorado is special.

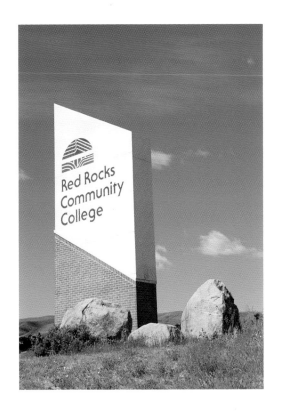

night. It is the change of seasons—sometimes all in one day. It is a fall that gives away to a glorious Indian summer. It is the variety of experiences available along the Front Range: playing

Above, left: Red Rocks Community College recognizes that the most important people in the College are the learners, and their needs drive the institution's decisions.

Above, right: Residents living in Jefferson County enjoy a mild climate where the sun shines year-round.

Left: Spectacular sunsets splash over Standley Lake.

golf on New Year's Day, skiing on the 4th of July. It's the outdoor spirit—hiking, biking, backpacking, picnicking, wildlife viewing. It's the well-planned trail system throughout the County. It's knowing that one can easily escape the city canyons of concrete for the green softness of a mountain side. It is the 255 days of sunshine and an average humidity of 38 percent.

But it is more than beautiful scenery and mild climate. It is normally mellow Westerners' passion about their way of life. It is the one-half percent sales tax to preserve open space. It is a diverse and competitive economy. It is the convenient access to higher educational institutions such as University of Colorado, Colorado School of Mines, and Red Rocks Community College.

Opposite: Colorado's natural beauty is enjoyed by cyclists.

Below: Jefferson County encourages an environment where development can make the cities better places to work and live.

Easy access to the mountains offers a wide range of recreational opportunities to Jefferson County residents.

It is the magic of live theater, music and dance. It is people who support the arts and love sports. It is a concert under the bright clear summer evening sky.

It is the Broncos, the Rockies, the Avalanche, the Nuggets and the Rapids. It is the 40 recreation centers. It is the Jefferson Symphony Orchestra and the Wheat Ridge Carnation Festival.

It is a high standard of living. It is highly skilled workers who could make the transition from an economy based upon mining and agriculture to one based on service.

It is the healthy Colorado lifestyle. It is the people and it is the land that will always define the quality of life in Jefferson County.

Jefferson County provides a diversity of housing, whether it be in the foothills or in a suburban community.

Right: Golden is a hang-glider and paraglider-friendly community.

Below: Sedimentary red rocks formed by wind, rain and frost dot the landscape as two bikers enjoy a ride.

Above: College students sharpen their soccer skills.

Left: Chatfield Reservoir offers summertime water activities for the entire family.

Right: Hiwan Golf Course is built on acres of mountain forests and meadows with challenging fairways. The ball drives ten percent farther at this altitude, making this a sharpshooter's dream!

Below: Jefferson County has a nationally recognized open space program that has so far preserved 29,000 acres of open space lands.

Left: A ribbon of I-70 provides spectacular scenery and easy access to year-round recreational opportunities in the Rocky Mountains.

Below: Long a Colorado landmark off I-70 and the Evergreen Parkway, El Rancho is a favorite family restaurant providing stunning views of the Rocky Mountains.

Top: Crown Hill has been kept in a natural state and is now home to a variety of wildlife including numerous species of waterfowl and shorebirds.

Above: Flowing through Golden, Clear Creek offers kayaking and river rafting opportunities while numerous hiking and walking trails line the banks of the river.

Opposite: Paragliders soar over the "M" on the face of Mount Zion. Since 1908, freshmen from the Colorado School of Mines have repainted the symbol in the fall.

A modern system of wind power, once an energy source of the frontier plains.

WHAT OF THE FUTURE?

Colorado and Jefferson County sit on the 105th meridian, midpoint between the Pacific Rim and Continental Europe. Here in the Mountain Time Zone, with the help of satellites throughout the world, it is possible to conduct business around the globe during the same eight-hour day. If the future is the information age, wired and technology savvy Jefferson County is ready.

The unique mix of natural and cultural amenities helps attract and retain highly-qualified professionals. Continuing the succession of knowledgeable workers started years ago, the area has the nation's second-highest rate of college graduates in the work force. With the skill levels of the population combined with the quality of everyday life,

Squiggles, a 343-foot-long "seasaurus" at the Arvada Center's playground has plenty of bends, folds and curves in which kids can climb and explore for hours.

Built in 1872 as the Golden Presbyterian Church, the Foothills Art Center houses a variety of fine art, sculpture and photography and conducts classes, lectures, workshops and art demonstrations.

Jefferson County is seen as an ideal place to live and work.

Nevertheless, Jefferson County is still Western at heart, and the people are ever mindful of the West's rich history—the efforts of miners, farmers, ranchers, and suppliers who worked hard and overcame hardships of the pioneer West. If there is a bump in the road, as there always has been in the history of Colorado, the way of the West will continue: work hard to refined the business climate while protecting the quality of life.

Governed by unpredictable weather and directed by the environment, the citizens of Jefferson County are self-reliant, dependable, hardworking. They've retained their work ethic

and sense inherited from the frontier beginnings. Optimistic about the future, their energies keep the business climate healthy.

The future remains in the traditions of the West: freedom, opportunity, and wide-open spaces in which to roam and dream. Jefferson County is uniquely positioned for the 21st century with digital infrastructure and wired communities, research facilities and technological achievements. The scenery, mild climate, commitment to a better life—and the central location. But the history of Jefferson County remains the land: what it was, what it will produce, and what it will support—and that will continue to tell the story of Jefferson County.

Parklands and open spaces near residential and commercial areas offer numerous opportunities for hiking and picnicking.

Above: Snow time is fun time.

*Right: Hikers rest on a scenic overlook to enjoy the benefits
of the mountains and plains environment.*

Below: Jefferson County, located in the mountain time zone, sits between Mexico and Canada, is equidistant to Europe and Asia, providing access to all national and international markets in the same business day.

The Westernairs, founded in 1949, is a nonprofit group that stresses precision riding, specialty teams, and horsemanship.

Left: The Lakewood Westernairs, a youth performance riding club, travels the nation and opens most local rodeos.

Bottom, left: Arvada Center for the Arts and Humanities offers a variety of year-round theatre, concerts, art galleries, and classes attracting more than 25,000 participants.

Below: One of the greatest draws of living and working in Jefferson County is the daily backdrop of both the high plains and the mountains from Turkey Creek Canyon.

*Above: Beginning in 1860,
railroads played a major role
in the economic development
of Jefferson County.*

*Right: The County has many
scenic open spaces with trails
for biking, hiking, running, and
in-line skating.*

Above: The Arvada Center for the Arts and Humanities is the only art and culture center in the area with all disciplines under one roof. The center is home to a 500-seat indoor theater and a 1,200-seat outdoor amphitheater.

Left: All Star Park, a youth baseball field, was launched by the Colorado Rockies as a way to give back to the community. The facility offers a championship-caliber playing surface and a giant scoreboard in left field similar to the one at Coors Field.

Above: Recreational baseball leagues focus on player participation and good sportsmanship.

Right: Magpies are among the most beautiful of Colorado birds most noted for their high-pitched, petulant calls which can be heard for long distances.

Opposite: Native plants continue to flourish in parks just a short ride from business areas.

Where there is a rapidly diversifying economy, there is growth.

Partners in Jefferson County

*Businesses and organizations that contribute
to the development and economic base
of Jefferson County*

FRIENDS

Bradley,
Campbell,
Carney &
Madsen, P.C.

Credit Union
of Denver

Evergreen
Memorial Park

Jehn &
Associates, Inc.

DENVER WEST REALTY, INC./ STEVINSON AUTOMOTIVE GROUP, INC.

Above: Greg Stevinson, President of Denver West Realty, Inc.

Below: Denver West Office Park is home to more than fifty technological and scientific companies in Jefferson County.

The Stevinson name has a long-time presence in Jefferson County. Starting in 1961 when Charles E. (Chuck) Stevinson opened his first automotive dealership at 13th and Ford Streets in Golden, the Stevinson name has come to symbolize business acumen and community responsibility. Chuck Stevinson and his family spent more than thirty-five years building an impressive assemblage of property development and automobile dealerships. Those entities (Stevinson Automotive Group, Inc. and Denver West Realty, Inc.) continue to flourish today under the leadership of Greg and Kent Stevinson. Kent Stevinson is president of Stevinson Automotive Group, Inc. and Greg Stevinson is president of Denver West Realty, Inc.

Greg Stevinson, as president of Denver West Realty Inc., is in charge of leasing for Denver West Office Park and master planning for the 750 acre land holding located at the confluence of five major highways in Jefferson County—I-70, U.S. 6, U.S. 40 (Colfax Avenue), Highway 93 and C-470.

Denver West Office Park occupies about 110 acres and currently has two million square feet of developed office space. More than fifty technological and scientific companies make their home in the Office Park, including the National Renewable Energy Laboratory (NREL); American Management Systems, one of the country's largest informa-

tion technology consulting firms; Aurum Software, a division of the Baan Company, one of the world's fastest growing business software providers; Rocky Mountain Remediation Services, a major subcontractor involved in the clean-up of Rocky Flats; ACT Teleconferencing, most recently in the national news because of their teamwork with AT&T in establishing the telemedicine link between climbers on Mount Everest and medical researchers at the Yale University School of Medicine and the MIT Media Lab.

Denver West Office buildings are designed in earth tones to blend with the surrounding environment. Lakes, streams, waterfalls, rustic bridges and mature foliage are landscaping details that add to the aesthetics and have helped the Office Park achieve national acclaim.

Greg heads the team responsible for the marketing and leasing of the twenty-seven building Office Park and the adjoining mixed-use development which includes a luxury 321 unit apartment complex called The Park at Denver West and a retail complex called Denver West Village.

Denver West Village, a 325,000 square foot shopping center opened in 1997. The Village includes tenants such as Bed, Bath & Beyond, Soundtrack, United Artists Theaters, Barnes & Noble Bookstore, Alfalfa's Market, Just For Feet, Old Navy, Christy Sports and

Office Max. Restaurants at the Village include: Tokyo Joe's, Z-Teca, Outback Steakhouse, On the Border and Macaroni Grill. Wendy's, Hops Grill & Bar and Mimis Café are the three newest additions.

The Village is the first of a two-phase shopping/entertainment recreation district. Phase two, a regional shopping district with major department store anchors, is being developed in partnership with TrizecHahn, the developer of Park Meadow Mall in Douglas County. A museum built to house the Harmsen Museum of Art is planned to be constructed as part of the shopping area.

Planning is also underway for a second phase of luxury apartment construction and patio home complex.

Stevinson Automotive Group leadership has been in the hands of Kent Stevinson since 1989 when his father chose him to oversee the brand new Lexus dealership. That appointment made Kent the youngest Lexus dealer in the nation. He assumed the title of president of the Automotive Group when Chuck passed away in 1995, but his involvement in the family business goes back to his earliest years.

Kent's automotive career started when he was eight years old sweeping the floors and dusting the parts bins at the dealership. After graduating from Arizona State University with a degree in accounting and economics, he

started working full-time in the business. For fifteen years, Kent labored in various positions: as an auditor, assistant used car manager and new car manager. He concentrated on the nuts and bolts of the business while the dealerships grew to include: Toyota West, Toyota East, Stevinson Chevrolet West, Stevinson Lexus, Stevinson Imports (Jaguar/Porsche), RV West and RV North. And in early 1997, Stevinson Automotive Group added the first Ford dealership to the Group by purchasing Golden Ford, one of the first car dealerships in the area, owned for forty-nine years by Ed Dubravac, a long-time family friend.

Both Greg and Kent Stevinson are actively involved in a wide range of community and organizational activities. Greg has been a member of the Jefferson County Open Space Advisory Committee (OSAC) for over nine years and to date has served as Chairman of OSAC for five terms. He has also served on the Board of Directors of the Red Rocks Community College Foundation and the West Chamber of Commerce. He is the former Chairman of the Board of Craig Hospital, a nationally recognized hospital specializing in the rehabilitation of patients with severe head and/or spinal injuries. He also served as a member of the Craig Hospital Foundation.

Above: Kent Stevinson, President of Stevinson Automotive Group, Inc.

Below: Denver West Village along I-70 and West Colfax Avenue.

Greg was a founder and director of Denver West Bank and Trust which eventually sold to Key Bank. He has served as a director and treasurer of the Jefferson Economic Council and was a founder and former director of the Colorado Business and Innovation Center. He serves on the Board of Trustees of the Midwest Research Institute and is a member of the Board of Trustees of Regis High School. In 1998, Greg was selected as one of four "Fathers of the Year" by the Juvenile Diabetes Foundation.

Kent, recognizing the strong support his family has received over the years, is equally involved in the community and eager to help organizations and charities that give back to the community. Stevinson's Golden Ford recently donated a truck for a raffle which raised more than $45,000 to benefit the Golden Visitors Center. Focusing on grassroots types of projects, Kent regularly schedules car washes at the dealerships to support schools, athletic programs and other worthy causes.

Stevinson Automotive Group has donated vehicles to other worthy causes; regularly sponsors golf tournaments that support local charities; funds a scholarship program at Warren Tech; contributes to the Christian Action Guild and the Golden Police Department's D.A.R.E. program. They have long sponsored the Denver Polo Classic which benefits the Robert R. McCormick Tribune Foundation. And, they sponsor a Rockies baseball clinic every year for local Little League teams. Kent was a founder of Denver 20/30 and has raised over $2 million for local children's charities. He is a member of the National Dealer Council for Jaguar Cars, Inc., the Lexus Dealer Council, and has served as the president of the Toyota Dealer Association and as a board member of the Denver Nuggets.

Greg Stevinson, Kent Stevinson, and the entire Stevinson family pledge that they will continue to be guided by the late Chuck Stevinson's credo: "You don't just take from a community—You give back."

Right: Stevinson Chevrolet located at Indiana Street and Colfax Avenue.

Below: Stevinson Lexus on Indiana Street in Golden.

RED ROCKS COMMUNITY COLLEGE

A caring student-centered learning environment draws some 13,000 different students to Red Rocks Community College annually. The 140 acre-main campus in Lakewood and satellite campuses in Arvada and Conifer combine natural beauty with electronic and state-of-the-art facilities that make classes available around the clock, every day.

The College, known for its commitment to access, learner-centered educational innovation and community outreach, specializes in learning opportunities for the working adult.

The Red Rocks Institute, co-located with the West Chamber of Commerce in the Denver West Office Park, is a resource for Jefferson County businesses needing short term, fast-track customized training for their employees. Since its inception in 1989, the Institute has served more than 12,000 employees from 145 businesses and agencies in 11 states. The Red Rocks Institute has helped companies like COBE Laboratories and Coors Brewing Company with on-site training centers.

The College's Computer Training Solutions 93, also located in the Denver West Office Park, provides technical training for area businesses. Individual, customized or group learning in programming, applications and networking.

The Red Rocks Weekend College is also designed specifically for the working adult. It is the only program in the area offering a business degree on weekends that can be earned in less than two years. Weekend class formats vary so that students can coordinate their work and school schedules. The classes are offered in small, intensive seminar forms to encourage networking, and they feature guest speakers and field experiences for workplace relevance.

"Real World" experiences are the hallmark of all the College's nearly 100 career certificate programs. Each is guided by an advisory committee comprising business professionals from throughout the region who help assure appropriate curricula to prepare students for jobs in various business sectors. This approach has resulted in unique and award-winning programs like Brewing Science Technology, Fire Science Technology, the OSHA Training Institute and the Red Rocks/Lutheran Health Careers Center which are extending Red Rocks' reputation not only regionally, but nationally and internationally as well.

Thirty-seven percent of all Red Rocks students are between the ages of 25 and 40, and 24 percent are over age 40. Fifteen percent have already completed at least a baccalaureate degree. Eighty-five percent of Red Rocks students work, and 27 percent are in work-related studies.

Red Rocks Community College is accredited by The Commission on Institutions of Higher Education of the North Central Association of Colleges and Schools. It is one of the fastest-growing institutions in the Colorado Community College and Occupational Education System which serves 72 percent of all college freshmen and sophomores in the state.

EXEMPLA HEALTHCARE

Exempla Lutheran Medical Center was founded in 1905 as the Evangelical Lutheran Sanatorium to treat tuberculosis patients. In 1962, it was converted to a full-service acute care hospital serving the Denver metropolitan area's rapidly growing west side.

Exempla Healthcare is the newest healthcare delivery system in town and, at the same time, it is the oldest. Formed January 1, 1998, Exempla Healthcare is comprised of Exempla Lutheran Medical Center, Exempla Saint Joseph Hospital and Exempla Medical Group. Jeffrey Selberg serves as president and chief executive officer of Exempla, and David Wollard serves as chairman of the board.

Given the date it was formed, Exempla's youth is obvious. But how can Exempla Healthcare also claim to be the oldest healthcare delivery organization in the Denver metropolitan area? Experience is the answer.

Exempla Saint Joseph Hospital opened its doors in September of 1873 and celebrated its 125th anniversary during 1998—the oldest private hospital in the area. Add to that the experience of Exempla Lutheran Medical Center, which has been caring for the citizens of the western metropolitan area and Jefferson County since 1905. The two hospitals were long-time friendly competitors when they decided in 1995 to collaborate by sponsoring a physician practice group that was originally called Primera Healthcare, now known as Exempla Medical Group.

By 1997, it seemed clear to the leadership of Exempla Saint Joseph Hospital, Exempla Lutheran Medical Center and Primera that a closer working relationship would enable them to make a stronger impact in improving community health. As a result, the three organizations integrated under one operating company, Exempla Healthcare. To understand the motivation to form the joint venture, it is helpful to understand something of the history of the two hospitals.

At the beginning of the twentieth century, tuberculosis was a serious health problem in the nation. Tuberculosis patients flocked to Colorado seeking a cure in this region's cool dry air. The Evangelical Lutheran Sanatorium, a forerunning predecessor to Exempla Lutheran, was established to provide care for tuberculosis patients. Over the years, the Sanatorium, which began as a tent colony, grew to a 100-bed hospital. By 1962, the demand for tuberculosis treatment had diminished, and community leaders converted the facility, located at 8300 West 38th Avenue, into Lutheran Hospital to meet the growing west metropolitan area healthcare needs. Other healthcare providers, such as Colorado

Lutheran Home and Homecare and Hospice, joined Lutheran Hospital to provide a full continuum of care, and the hospital was soon reorganized as Lutheran Medical Center.

Exempla Saint Joseph Hospital was founded by the Sisters of Charity of Leavenworth to care for Denver's sick and needy when Denver was a fast-growing frontier city. The Catholic hospital was established in a rented cottage but soon outgrew that space and several other rented facilities. Its permanent home was established in 1876 on the ground it occupies today between Franklin and Humboldt Streets at 18th Avenue. The Sisters of Charity of Leavenworth, a sponsoring organization of Exempla, operated the hospital until Exempla assumed management in 1998. Under Exempla's management, Saint Joseph Hospital continues to adhere to the Catholic healthcare directives.

Both hospitals were started to meet a need in the community, and, as not-for-profit organizations, both have remained strongly grounded in the community. Exempla Healthcare, was formed to continue the work of its two founding organizations. Its mission statement reads in part: "Exempla will deliver healthcare that is integrated for the good of the people we serve and responsive to improving the health of the community with special concern for the underserved."

Because of its commitment to improving community health, Exempla is dedicated to working closely with physicians to determine the health needs of the community. Six physicians serve on Exempla's thirteen-member Board of Directors. Highly involved is Exempla Medical Group, a large primary-care physician group with practices throughout the metropolitan region.

In complying with its mission, Exempla Healthcare forms cooperative relationships with a variety of community groups and organizations, including the Colorado Xplosion, the professional women's basketball team, Mile High Girl Scouts, Congregational Health Partners, The Gathering Place, and others, to provide health education and wellness programs.

In addition, Exempla offers a variety of health education programs and management

services to the community. Many programs are free, while others charge nominal fees.

Exempla Lutheran Medical Center and Exempla Saint Joseph Hospital are two of metropolitan Denver's most respected hospitals and are known throughout the region for providing low cost, quality care. Both hospitals have been named to the list of 100 Top Hospitals in the United States compiled by two healthcare consulting companies, Mercer Management Consulting and HCIA, Inc. Each has been named to the list three of the last five years, the only Colorado hospitals to achieve such consistent recognition.

Both Exempla Saint Joseph Hospital and Exempla Lutheran Medical Center are general acute care hospitals but are also known for their leadership in certain specialty areas of care, particularly women's health, cardiovascular, oncology, and orthopedic services.

Exempla Healthcare is proud of its long commitment to the Denver metropolitan community. As a new healthcare system, the organization's 5,800 employees, 2,000 physicians and hundreds of volunteers look forward to leading the community with the kind of healthcare it needs and expects in the twenty-first century.

Exempla Saint Joseph Hospital was founded in 1873 and is the oldest private teaching hospital in Colorado with residency programs training physicians in Family Practice Medicine, Internal Medicine, Obstetrics and Gynecology, and Surgery.

TMJ
Implants, Inc.

Above: Lynne and Robert
Christensen.

Below: The Christensen Fossa-
Eminence and Condylar
Prostheses for reconstruction of the
temporomandibular joint.

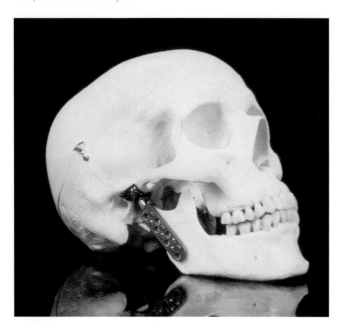

Dr. Robert Christensen, President of TMJ Implants, Inc., is a man with a passion for assisting others and whose living legacy will continue to touch the hearts of many people for years to come. As an inventor, doctor, professor, author and minister, Dr. Christensen has accomplished more than most individuals dream could happen in a lifetime.

Dr. Christensen received his D.D.S. degree from New York University in 1948, graduating Cum Laude. Following graduation, he trained as a graduate resident in oral surgery at Los Angeles County General Hospital, then joined the U.S. Navy for a short time. In 1953, Dr. Christensen began his private practice as an oral and maxillo-facial surgeon. He practiced in Pasadena, Lawndale and northern California until his retirement from active practice in 1988. In that time period, he also served as an Assistant Clinical Professor of Head and Neck Surgery at the University of California, School of Medicine at Irvine.

In 1988, Dr. Christensen and his wife, Lynne, founded TMJ Implants, Inc. Today, TMJ Implants and two sister companies are international leaders in prostheses technology and anatomical modeling.

Dr. Christensen's pioneering efforts in the field of dental and temporomandibular joint implants led to a unique development over three decades ago, the Christensen Fossa-Eminence and Condylar Prostheses for reconstruction of the temporomandibular joint. Due to the irreversible progression of temporomandibular joint disease (TMJ), a disorder of the jaw, the joints in many patients cannot be repaired. Instead, they must be replaced through partial or total joint reconstruction. Dr. Christensen's advanced, yet simple, prostheses prevent the destruction of bone and reduce the possibility of soft tissue injury. They also prevent the likelihood of patients needing to endure repeat surgery. But it is the people Dr. Christensen has helped who tell the real story.

Jamie, a young woman from Florida, had been suffering from weekly migraine headaches since she was seven years old. As a

nurse, she did not think she had TMJ because her jaw did not "click" or "pop," a common symptom of TMJ sufferers. Surgical replacement of her right TM Joint with a Christensen prosthesis was performed, and Jamie has been relieved of her weekly headaches.

A Littleton resident, Charlene, suffered for fifteen years with a dull nagging pain in her temple. Pain in her jaw worsened and eventually reduced her to living on broth, malts, baby food and gelatin. In 1990, after four unsuccessful surgeries, Charlene had a Fossa-Eminence Prosthesis implanted on each side of her jaw. She felt better within the week and immediately noticed the huge improvement the prostheses made to her daily life. No longer restricted by food, Charlene's life has returned to normal.

Overwhelming examples of similar successes abound. Patients are amazed at the quick recovery time and the significant reduction of pain after surgery. Within days, patients are enjoying the ability to speak, eat and chew, many for the first time in years.

This level of comfort and success is possible by the precise matching of the prosthesis to the anatomical nuances of the patient's jaw. Recently, the accuracy of the implant's fit has been greatly improved with the introduction of computer-aided design (CAD) and the manufacturing of anatomical models. Hence, the development of a sister company to TMJ Implants, Medical Modeling Corporation.

Developed in 1995, Medical Modeling Corporation is overseen by General Manager Andrew Christensen, one of Dr. Christensen's

sons. The company creates precision models of TMJ patients' facial bone structures, using stereolithography rapid prototyping equipment. In final form, each model furnishes a template for diagnosing and planning treatment for surgery. This results in a prosthesis that is perfectly suited to each individual. Having the model allows a doctor to thoroughly explain the surgical procedure to the patient, enhancing lines of communication. It also aids in discussing options with surgical team members, simulating an operating procedure before surgery, and in making adjustments during last-minute surgical preparation. As a result, the implant procedure is more effective and the outcome more predictable for the patient.

The versatility of the modeling process has prompted its use in many other reconstructive applications. Not only is the process used in temporomandibular joint or mandibular reconstruction, it is being used by orthopedic surgeons for hip, knee, shoulder, finger, ankle and elbow reconstruction and by otolaryngologists and plastic surgeons for facial reconstructive surgery.

In May 1998, Medical Modeling Corporation became the first company in the nation to produce sterilizable ClearView™ anatomical models. This places the company well ahead in the field of providing computed tomography-based models. The material is in use in four companies worldwide that provide patient-specific anatomical modeling services.

The ClearView™ anatomical models are high-temperature steam autoclavable, which allows for last minute sterilization prior to surgery. Selective coloration gives the surgeon a more accurate view of localized areas to treat. Both the ability to sterilize and selectively color anatomical models give surgeons more flexibility than ever before, especially during surgery.

A second company, Design

Above: Patient specific implant constructed on stereolithography model.

Below: Robert and Andrew Christensen with enlarged stereolithography model of patient's skull.

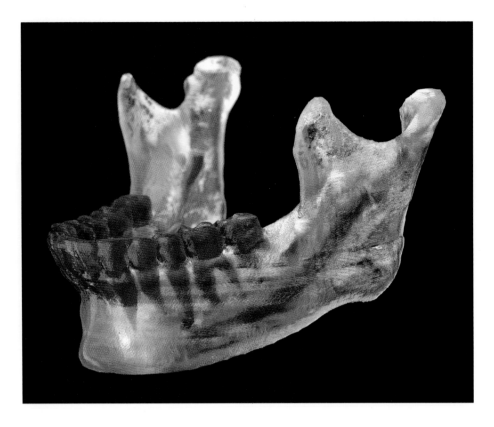

Above: Stereolithography model of patient's lower jaw with coloration of teeth and neurovascular bundle.

Below: Dr. Christensen and co-host Pastor Ron Griego (far left) with guests on Building The Kingdom In Families television program.

University School of Engineering for Dr. Christensen's contributions and advancement of science. He has been honored through the University of Tennessee Medical Center at Knoxville for his support of products and services for oral and maxillofacial surgery patients. In 1996, the Robert W. Christensen TMJ Surgery Chair Fellowship was started to further research and teaching in TMJ disease. In addition, Dr. Christensen is listed in *Who's Who in the World*, *Who's Who in America*, *Who's Who in the West*, *Who's Who in Medicine and Healthcare*, and *Who's Who in Science and Engineering*.

Dr. Christensen's willingness to aid those around him does not stop with his accomplishments in the dental and medical arena, however. He is also the founder and Pastor of Covenant Marriages Ministry, part of the business complex housing TMJ Implants, Medical Modeling Corporation and Design Dynamics International.

Covenant Marriages Ministry focuses on the sacredness of the marriage covenant and declares marriage as a life-long committed relationship. Dr. Christensen was called to the ministry in 1983 and has since shared his message throughout the United States as well as in the Ukraine, Spain, Netherlands, Israel and Bermuda. As an ordained minister, Dr. Christensen co-hosts the television series *Building The Kingdom In Families* with Ronald Griego, a pastor, teacher and writer. The television series is seen daily in Denver, Albuquerque and Memphis. It is also shown weekly in Alaska and Arkansas as well as being on Sky Angel Satellite. Another of Dr. Christensen's sons, Matthew, works in the graphic department and in television production for the ministry and TMJ Implants.

In addition to their pastoral and TV ministries, Dr. Christensen and Pastor Griego conduct seminars on marriage healing and restoration in churches all across America. Their gift for assisting individuals and couples in need has brought tremendous joy and healing to the lives of many.

TMJ Implants, Inc. and Covenant Marriages Ministry, under the leadership of Dr. Robert Christensen, are enterprises that have progressed to heights of which legacies are made. Not just in the eyes of Jefferson County residents, but to people all over the world.

Dynamics International, Inc., was developed in 1996. The company manufactures precision metal products such as: surgical screws, parts for casting reels, parts for bicycles, and many other products, using state-of-the-art Swiss screw machines.

Dr. Christensen, TMJ Implants and its sister companies have received numerous awards and recognition over the years. In September 1997, the Robert W. Christensen Bio-mechanical Laboratory was established at Clemson

In 1931, Credit Union of Denver became the third credit union chartered in Colorado. It was formed to offer its members, employees of federal government agencies, a wide range of valuable financial services. Since that time, Credit Union of Denver has expanded to over 31,000 members. Their membership also includes veterans of foreign wars who live in Colorado and their family members, members of over 250 Select Employee Groups (SEGs), select area high school and college students, and individuals who have reached 54+ years of age living or working in Jefferson County. While membership, in some instances, spans beyond the Colorado boundaries, members remain committed to the loyal service provided by Credit Union of Denver.

Today, Credit Union of Denver manages nearly $200 million in assets and is federally insured by the National Credit Union Administration (NCUA).

Like all credit unions, Credit Union of Denver is a member-owned, not-for-profit, cooperative. Any profits incurred are returned to the membership through higher deposit rates and dividends, lower loan rates and improved services.

On the forefront of service technology, Credit Union of Denver was one of the first Colorado credit unions to offer its members access to their accounts via the Internet. This service is in addition to its 24-hour a day telephone account access and loan application capabilities. Currently in the process of opening a cashless branch at the Tivoli, Credit Union of Denver remains committed to pro-

viding state-of-the-art services to meet the needs of its members.

Credit Union of Denver is a member of the West Chamber and is highly active in the Jefferson County community. The credit union offers a variety of paid internship positions, donates to the Jefferson County Action Center, Front Range Cycle and Colorado Christian Home, and contributes to a number of high school and college scholarship programs. These schools include Arvada West High School, Chatfield Senior High School, Green Mountain Senior High School, Colorado Christian College, Community College of Denver, Metropolitan State College of Denver and Red Rocks Community College. Children's Hospital is also a recipient of the credit union's efforts through annual sponsor-

ship of the Courage Classic and Link Up.

Credit Union of Denver is dedicated to being a leader in providing quality financial service, exceeding members' expectations and achieving a loyal relationship among members, staff and the community.

Above: Main branch conveniently located at the corner of Alameda Parkway and Garland Street in Lakewood.

Below: A leader in the industry's technology, Credit Union of Denver offers a variety of account access options for members.

KAISER-HILL COMPANY, LLC

Top: An aerial view of Rocky Flats.

Bottom: Building 123, a 19,000 square-foot former analytical laboratory, is demolished.

Opposite, top: A worker checks a furnace inside of a glovebox used to process plutonium residues into a more stable form for storage.

Opposite, middle: Workers examine a drum containing depleted uranium chips unearthed from Trench 1, a top-10 hazardous substance site cleaned up by the Kaiser-Hill team.

Opposite, bottom: More than 200 head of mule deer can be found living in the Rocky Flats Buffer Zone.

Brought together to address the cleanup challenges posed by the Department of Energy's (DOE) Rocky Flats Environmental Technology Site, a former nuclear weapons production facility, Kaiser-Hill Company is a joint venture of two of the world's leading environmental and engineering firms—ICF Kaiser and CH2M HILL.

ICF Kaiser is one of the largest engineering, construction and consulting service companies in the United States. Headquartered in Fairfax, Virginia, ICF Kaiser employs more than 5,000 professionals in twenty-five countries on six continents who tackle projects ranging from Superfund site cleanup to multibillion-dollar construction projects.

Denver-based CH2M HILL is one of the nation's largest environmental engineering firms with experience at defense installations, DOE sites and commercial facilities. With revenues topping $1 billion, CH2M HILL provides consulting, design, construction, operating and systems integration services, and employs 7,500 people in 120 offices worldwide.

Kaiser-Hill was awarded the integrating management contract for the Rocky Flats Closure Project in April, 1995, and assumed operations of the 6,300-acre site on July 1 of the same year. Located in northwest Jefferson County, Rocky Flats once housed more than fourteen tons of plutonium and seven and one-half tons of uranium—more than any other DOE manufacturing facility.

Nearly forty years of nuclear weapons production at Rocky Flats left behind a legacy of radioactive waste and environmental contamination. With no further weapons production mission, the goal today is to clean up the site, demolish the facilities and close Rocky Flats down forever. When Kaiser-Hill was awarded the contract, initial projections showed cleanup would take seventy years and cost as much as $36 billion. Within three months of the contract's start, the project was restructured under a plan that could be executed for $6 billion spent over ten years.

The overall Rocky Flats Closure Project is now being performed as a series of projects encompassing five major elements: Special Nuclear Material stabilization, packaging and consolidation; deactivation, decommissioning and demolition; environmental restoration; property and records disposition; and offsite shipment.

The project scope is truly daunting. For example, more than 700 facilities must be dismantled, 640,000 items of property must be removed, 154,500 cubic meters of contaminated waste must be shipped offsite, and dozens of contaminated environmental sites must be cleaned up. Throughout the cleanup process, Kaiser-Hill emphasizes the safety of site workers and protection of the public and the environment.

Kaiser-Hill, working in close coordination with the DOE and Rocky Flats stakeholders, has assembled a team of best-in-class companies to address these challenges. Kaiser-Hill's contract at Rocky Flats was one of the first awarded under the DOE's contract reform initiative. Under this contract, Kaiser-Hill assigns and integrates tasks among several main subcontractor companies, who in turn contract with hundreds of specialty subcontractors—each with expertise in a project area.

The DOE Rocky Flats Field Office performs direct oversight of the contract at Rocky Flats with additional oversight from DOE headquarters in Washington, D.C. All project activities are regulated by the Colorado Department of Public Health and Environment and the U.S. Environmental Protection Agency. The Rocky Flats Cleanup Agreement, signed on July 19, 1996, governs cleanup activities at Rocky Flats. Nuclear activities also fall under the oversight of the Defense Nuclear Facilities Safety Board.

By cleaning up and closing down Rocky Flats, Kaiser-Hill is making Jefferson County safer for future generations. Successful closure of the site will remove a major environmental risk from the Front Range area and will return a valuable parcel of property—more than 6,000 acres—for other future use. Together, Kaiser-Hill employees are moving toward their goal to "Make it safe. Clean it up. Close it down."

SALCO, INC.

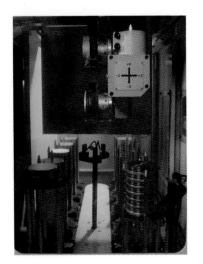

Precision engineering and machining are synonymous with the name SALCO, Inc. A locally owned and operated company driven by an ambitious goal to be the best precision machined parts manufacturer in the global marketplace.

SALCO, Inc. was founded in 1985. Today, Bob Salvatore and his wife, Irene, originally from Trinidad, Colorado, remain committed to their original philosophy which includes providing a personal touch to business relationships and maintaining a team commitment among employees, staff members and customers.

Over the years, the Salvatore's have remained true to their company's vision.

When asked to elaborate on that vision, Bob and Irene say they want each worker to be part of their family where individual efforts are both noticed and rewarded. They also want to establish more than just a business relationship or partnership with customers. This genuine team focus creates the heart of SALCO's success. Employees and customers alike will attest to the Salvatore's full commitment to this unique philosophy which is paying off today.

The adherence to the Salvatore's personal philosophy is also evident through the involvement of Bob and Irene's two sons in the company. Dino handles the quoting and customer contact while Joe takes care of the manufacturing operations. The combined talents of Bob, Dino and Joe provide SALCO with over fifty years of machining expertise. This experience, along with the dedication of SALCO's nearly fifty employees and management staff members, has helped the company create a strong winning team of which all are proud to be a part.

Employees at SALCO take great pride in their responsibilities. With access to quality equipment and material, understanding and support from management, and flexibility in overall work schedules, employees are eager to collaborate to create better and faster ways to manufacture parts while maintaining the highest of standards and cost effectiveness for both the company and its customers.

SALCO manufactures parts for the aero-

space, medical, pump, spray and computer industries, utilizing materials such as aluminum, brass, copper, stainless steel, titanium and a variety of plastics. Parts range in size from the head of a pin used in computer equipment, often as small as .0325 of an inch up to forty-eight inch plates. The company's impressive customer base includes Hewlett-Packard, Ball Aerospace, Denver Instruments, Parker Hannifin, Binks Sames, OEA, and many other large corporations seeking the company's hand-in-hand commitment and dedication to its services.

SALCO relies entirely on its reputation for obtaining new customers. As a result, the company utilizes no advertising or sales staff. Upon touring SALCO's attractive 18,000 square foot facility, potential customers see first-hand its cleanliness, organizational flow and state-of-the-art capabilities. A new customer's decision is typically made, on the spot to integrate and become part of SALCO's elite team approach in providing them with quality end-products.

Located in Arvada, Colorado, SALCO houses thirty pieces of high-end CNC equipment. Each piece of equipment was purchased with a single objective in mind—to have available the necessary machinery to meet the unique and various needs of its customers. This diversity in equipment represents SALCO's ability to handle requests for processes that require CNC Swiss style screw machining, CNC milling, CNC turning and Automatic transfer machining. In addition, the company's extensive support equipment confirms SALCO's ongoing commitment to provide each customer with one-stop machin-

ing service from prototype to production runs.

Keeping track of SALCO's people, equipment and work requests can be an overwhelming task. Ask any staff member and he or she will gladly expound on the efficiency created by one of the most state-of-the-art manufacturing software systems available. Vista software, developed by DataWorks Corporation, provides SALCO with scheduling, quoting, purchase orders, tracking, inventory and accounting on every job, as well as machine, operation and employee information at any moment. Having this up-to-the-minute analysis and reporting allows management to make informed decisions almost instantaneously on nearly any aspect of work.

In 1995, SALCO was recognized by the City of Arvada as the Outstanding Business of the Year. In 1996, it was presented the Industry Recognition Award by Jefferson County. The company has also been recognized for its efforts in environmental safety by the City of Westminster.

As a company that used no hazardous materials, SALCO serves as an example for quality waste water management. Yet, the highest honor awarded the company by its employee's standards, is the repeat business that results from a job well done. No wonder SALCO, Inc.'s success is measured by its strong commitment; a focus which allows everyone to be successful.

Above: This 6 axis CNC Lathe makes complex parts complete while eliminating the need for any milling operations.

Below: SALCO holds tolerances up to .0002 and can meet cosmetic requirements up to a 16 finish.

THE CONSOLIDATED MUTUAL WATER COMPANY

Maple Grove Dam and Reservoir, 1956 and 1986.

In the early 1900's, suburban living began to develop in portions of east central Jefferson County. A number of people working in Denver found it pleasant and desirable to live west of the city. With easy access to this area made possible by an electric interurban line between Denver and Golden and the increasing availability of automobiles, the area quickly began to grow.

During this time, water was east central Jefferson County's primary concern. Homes and businesses were supplied only by individual surface wells, leaving the quality of the water less than desirable and detracting from what was otherwise considered pleasant suburban life. However, the problem was not insurmountable. Neighborly cooperation quickly came into play. Groups of three or four neighbors began pooling their resources and drilled new wells into deep underground aquifers some 600 to 700 feet below the surface. They built small pumphouses and wooden storage tanks, laid pipe to their homes and, presto—miniature water systems were in place! But as with any rapid growth, new problems arose, and the neighborhood systems needed to be combined. They were eventually incorporated into nonprofit, mutual water companies.

In June 1926, four of these small companies (Oaks Mutual Water, North Wadsworth Mutual Water, Glen Creighton Mutual Water and Wadsworth Mutual Water) were merged into The Consolidated Mutual Water Company, giving Denver's westerly suburbs a single company large enough to successfully administer and provide quality water service to the area.

The depression and drought in the early 1930's resulted in the need for more change. The water table was being depleted, the wood-stave tanks were drying out and precious water was leaking away. In 1932, Consolidated Mutual Water reorganized and its new Board negotiated an agreement with the Denver Water Board to purchase Denver water, which was the best alternative at the time. The cost of the new eight-inch water line and connection was $30,000. With no money in the treasury, assessments were imposed on the 600 stockholders/users, who either paid $50 in cash or worked out their assessment by digging the trench for the new line. Soon Denver water was flowing, faucets were gurgling, and Consolidated Mutual Water was prospering.

Then, in 1951, the historical "Blue Line" was established. This meant the Denver Water Board would not supply water beyond this "Blue Line" limit into metropolitan areas.

Water from Denver had increasingly become the major supply for Consolidated, and the use of deep wells was not considered to be a reliable long-term source. Faced with water rationing and increasing demands for water service west of the "Blue Line," an area

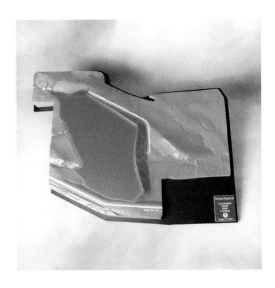

of rapid growth, Consolidated began acquiring surface water rights and constructed the Maple Grove Reservoir and Treatment Plant, which were completed in 1957. These facilities eventually displaced the remaining deep wells, providing a more reliable and less costly water supply. Today, the Maple Grove Plant provides approximately 30% of the company's annual water requirements with the other 70% still being purchased from Denver.

Ten other water systems have joined Consolidated since the initial merger in 1926. The company continues to follow the original pattern of the early cooperatives—ownership by the water users. The number of water taps within the system has increased from 136 to 20,228 as of late January 1998, providing service to an estimated 85,000 people within a 27 square mile service area of Lakewood, Wheat Ridge and east central Jefferson County through a network of 359 miles of pipeline.

Consolidated's office is located on the northwest shoreline of the Maple Grove Reservoir at 12700 West 27th Avenue in Lakewood and contains nearly 19,000 square feet of office space, 21,000 square feet of garage space, and 7,000 square feet of warehouse space.

The Treatment Plant, which is very important to the continuing delivery of high-quality water to the stockholders, has been expanded physically and technologically over the years in several increments from the original two million gallon-per-day capacity to its current capacity of 12 million gallons per day.

The Maple Grove Reservoir was enlarged in 1985 by removing approximately one million cubic yards of earth, increasing the facility's raw-water storage capacity to 1103 acre-feet of water (about 359 million gallons). A second raw-water storage reservoir, the Fairmount Reservoir at West 46th Avenue and McIntyre Street, was completed in 1993 and is capable of impounding 995 acre-feet of water (about 324 million gallons). A third reservoir will be located northwest of the Highway 72 and Indiana Street intersection. By far the largest of Consolidated's reservoirs, the new reservoir will have a capacity of 9,000 acre-feet of water (approximately 2.9 billion gallons) and is expected to be in service by 2005.

The founders of Consolidated Mutual were correct in their vision for creating a strong, mutual organization for the benefit of the surrounding community. Today's combination of a contract to purchase water from Denver and the independent Maple Grove System have resulted in one of the finest water systems in suburban metropolitan Denver. That system will further improve as Consolidated Mutual Water Company continues to replace, enlarge and enhance its water treatment, distribution and operating systems to accommodate Jefferson County's future growth and expansion.

Above: Future reservoir at Highway 72 and Indiana Street.

Below: Fairmount Reservoir, 1993.

ASPHALT PAVING COMPANY

Above: Quarry entrance on Highway 93 north of Golden.

Below: Main office in Golden, Colorado.

From the roads and runways at Denver International Airport to the top of Vail Pass, including many local highways and area subdivisions in between, if you live in or have visited Denver, you've driven on some of the best paving work in the area.

Asphalt Paving Company, located in Golden, was founded in 1955 by John H. Keller. Mr. Keller's vision was to build a company that would provide jobs and be an enterprise that could be passed along through the family. Three generations later, Asphalt Paving Company remains a family owned business carrying on Mr. Keller's original vision and is dedicated to maintaining the highest standard of quality workmanship in the industry.

For many years, John H. Keller operated Asphalt Paving Company with a primary focus on offering local paving services. John's son, Bill, was involved in the business from early on. Then, in 1968, wanting to venture out on his own, Bill created a company called Keller Construction Company which focused on building bridges and providing curb and gutter. Keller Construction Company operated independently of Asphalt Paving, working as a subcontractor to the asphalt company as needed.

Upon retiring in 1970, John H. Keller sold most of the assets of Asphalt Paving. In 1971, Bill purchased the company name which led to its rebirth. Today, Bill's oldest son, Jeff, serves as president of the firm while his second son, John, serves as president of a Summit County location. With a strong family base, Asphalt Paving Company remains a great contributor to the Colorado economy, particularly in the Jefferson County region.

Asphalt Paving Company is a full-service construction and aggregate mining/processing business as well as a materials supplier. The company produces a wide variety of high quality aggregates, unequaled in strength and durability, for both functional and aesthetic uses. From roadways and parking lots to furnace and fireplace linings and facias, Asphalt Paving mines and produces the best aggregate in the area, mostly from a quarry located just north of Golden on Highway 93.

Highly concerned about the environment, Asphalt Paving Company goes to great lengths to conserve natural resources and to protect the area's ecosystem. Portable asphalt plants allow for on-site processing whenever possible. Recycling existing pavement into

new work, reclamation of aggregate mining areas, and the use of state-of-the-art pollution control equipment at all production facilities are just a few examples of how Asphalt Paving ensures it is part of an environmental solution rather than a contributor to the problem.

Considered a 'small' company compared to its competition, Asphalt Paving employs nearly 200 people depending on the workload and the industry's seasonal demands. However, for a 'small' company, it has a big reputation with national recognition. Walk through the main office at 14802 West 44th Avenue and you will see trophies and awards honoring the company for its dedication to quality work and interest in helping others achieve. Asphalt Paving Company has received numerous local and national awards for its workmanship, partnering ability, high integrity and innovation. The company tends to bid on and is awarded those jobs that are more difficult to complete which in turn ranks them at the top of their industry throughout the United States. For example, in 1984, Asphalt Paving Company undertook the first specified night paving job in the Denver area, receiving recognition for its quality workmanship. The company takes pride in being able to supply materials and having the experience to handle new, innovative jobs and those that require stringent specifications or even experimental materials.

Other awards to Asphalt Paving Company's credit include: the National Asphalt Pavement Association's (NAPA) Overlay Award, the second most prestigious award in the United States, for resurfacing a portion of I-70 to Floyd Hill; the Golden Oldies Award in recognition of paving work along Highway 58 that lasted 23 years without needing additional repair; a national Excellence in Partnering Award for the company's commitment, contributions and cooperation while working with other subcontractors to complete joint projects; as well as honors for excellence in construction, workforce development and compliance to stringent safety standards.

In conjunction with its involvement in local and national trade associations, Asphalt Paving Company is known throughout the community for its longtime sponsorship of area youth programs such as basketball, baseball and football leagues, and most recently, the Junior Drag Racing National Championships. Furthermore, Asphalt Paving continues to actively support many philanthropic causes at both the local and national levels.

A family dedicated to helping other families build strong working ties, Asphalt Paving Company is a trusted name in its industry and the Jefferson County community.

Above: E-470 Design/Build contract—New pavement by Asphalt Paving Company.

Below: Loaded trucks at quarry ready to head to a job site.

SAS CIRCUITS, INC.

Right: Visual and dimensional inspection verifies customer requirements are satisfied prior to shipment.

Below: Printing of customer's circuit design.

Bottom: Automated Optical Inspection (AOI).

SAS Circuits, Inc., a closely held Colorado Corporation, was founded in July 1984. An acronym for its founders, Richard Snogren, Wayne Ardinger and Herb Snogren, SAS is located at 10570 Bradford Road in Littleton.

SAS Circuits manufactures high technology printed wiring boards (PWBs), the interconnecting foundation of all electronic devices. With diverse capabilities in a broad range of product applications, the company's manufacturing processes meet both government and commercial specifications. Over the years, SAS has produced PWBs for communication satellites, galaxy exploring devices, antennas, navigational and directional equipment, as well as for medical instruments, gaming machines, radar and power distribution equipment, readers, scanners, printers, plotters, instrumentation and many other applications.

SAS started operations in a 2,600 square foot leased space near its current headquarters. Herb began purchasing equipment while Richard, Wayne and their spouses, built fur-

niture and workbenches during evenings and on weekends. Initially, the company laminated and drilled multi-layer boards (MLBs) as a service to local PWB manufacturing shops, none of which made MLBs at the time. In a few months, SAS began manufacturing complete MLBs and quickly moved beyond the lamination and drilling service business.

Since its inception, SAS has steadily grown. Its niche market has expanded from quick-turn prototypes to include quick-turn limited production, and its technology has grown from basic commercial PWBs to leading-edge, high reliability products. SAS now occupies a 30,000 square foot company-owned facility. Expansion took place in several phases, increasing machine capacity thirty-fold and operating capacity twenty-fold since original production began. Today, SAS employs 130 people and operates around the clock.

The company is known for meeting the demanding project schedules of its clients, where time to market is critical. Turnaround for prototype quantities of PWBs can be as quick as twenty-four hours, with limited production in as few as five days. It's little wonder that customer satisfaction is listed as one of the key success factors of SAS Circuits.

The SAS team follows a total quality management philosophy. Together, team members dedicate their resources to support their internal and external customers' special needs by consistently manufacturing and delivering, on-time, the highest quality printed wiring products available. The company's commitment to building honest, mutually beneficial

relationships among team members, and with internal and external customers, suppliers, the government and the environment, has gained SAS the reputation of being a national leader in its chosen market niche.

SAS Circuits is committed to its surrounding community. In addition to a strong and steady employment rate, SAS sponsors a yearly program to assist families and children in need. This venture is coordinated by the company's FUNd Team, a group of energetic workers whose mission is to "promote communication and a sense of family through social activities among SAS employees and the community." Also, coordinated by the health and environmental affairs staff, SAS informs the surrounding area about the proper handling of manufacturing materials. The company dedicates over 400 community hours a year to these causes. For these and other efforts, SAS received industry recognition in 1994 and 1998 for contributing to the economic growth in Jefferson County.

With the increasing demand for smaller, denser and lower cost interconnections on PWBs, new technologies beyond conventional PWBs must be developed. Without advancement in technologies, the PWB industry will not be able to economically produce the interconnections required to meet the electronic industry's demands. SAS is responding to this need by rapidly developing microvia technology to enable production of high density, low cost interconnections. By developing these processes for creating small-

er via holes, smaller lines and tighter spaces, SAS now can economically produce smaller and tighter interconnections. The company also has the capability of producing PWB products from virtually all high performance dielectric substrate materials. These and other leading-edge technologies are what make SAS a leader in PWB technology.

PWBs are a major and critical component of today's overall electronics market; a market that expands well beyond the computer industry. With the PWB market expected to increase between 15% and 22% per year through 2001, SAS projects its annual sales to be over $20 million shortly after the turn of the century. That's good news for SAS Circuits Inc., its employees and Jefferson County.

PIPER ELECTRIC COMPANY, INC.

*Above: Optima Batteries, Inc.
World Headquarters and
Production Facility in Aurora,
Colorado.*

*Below: Automated production line
installed by Piper Electric at
Optima Batteries, Inc.*

Piper Electric Company, Inc. evolved from the business philosophies of its founding partners Gary Brown and Robert Piper. Their philosophies included principles that remain the focal point for the company today and help guide Piper Electric toward its goal of maintaining a top reputation throughout the construction and business community. With an ever-evolving vision—building lasting relationships and careers through innovative team performance—Piper Electric continues to lead its industry in providing both engineering and construction in one full-service operation.

Piper Electric started in 1983 in Bob Piper's garage. After a few short months, the company moved to a small unit in an office/warehouse complex on West 52nd Avenue in Arvada. As pioneers in Design/Build, the small staff of four quickly grew to twelve as the business community learned about their unique capabilities in providing electrical engineering and related services.

With an increase in staff, an inevitable move was on the horizon. Piper Electric searched for new office space and found a one acre parcel of land just down the road with a small house and two ramshackle outbuildings. After a great deal of clean up, employees moved into the house in 1984 with Marsha Young, Terry Ann Taylor and Bob Piper running the office out of the "front rooms", Gary Brown claiming work space in one of the bedrooms and Dave Doherty taking over the kitchen. The "warehouse" consisted of two trailers parked side-by-side and was conveniently located out the back door. Jo Ann Brown soon joined the team as a draftsperson; CAD was still a futuristic concept. An enclosed porch became her office where she claims to have done her best drawings because of the many windows and natural light.

Clientele grew rapidly, and in 1990, Piper Electric moved once again. This time to its

current location at 5960 Jay Street. Initially, the company occupied only a small portion of the building, approximately 2000-square feet. Today, Piper claims the entire 14,500-square foot complex to accommodate its forty office employees and 130 electricians and technicians. The facility is fully networked with fax and computer access to all major project sites. CAD drawings are the norm, and Piper Electric is winning national awards for its completion of high tech projects.

Included in Piper's facility is the company's own Career Development Center for in-house training. With the rapid changes in today's construction business, Piper makes education a priority by providing leadership, management, technical, sales and marketing training to its employees. In addition, the company offers its clients' employees the education and support they need to understand, run and maintain their own automated production systems. Piper's Career Development Center, a unique feature in the contracting industry, is part of the company's continuing evolution as a leading provider of high tech services.

Satisfied customers abound on Piper Electric's client list. Whether service is large or small, for a new or long-time client, Piper focuses on delivering quality work, on time

and within budget. Its combined disciplines and strong team approach among employees allow the company to provide a complete range of services that is second to none.

Trust and teamwork are the themes that run through the comments clients make about Piper Electric. Outstanding service, excellence, quality, commitment, cooperation, knowledgeable, and responsive are just a few of the words used to describe the work completed by the company and its staff. With strong commitment to serving the customer, employees focus on making a Piper client a client for life.

Landmark projects to Piper's credit include Geneva Pharmaceuticals, Volant Ski, Bolder Technologies Corporation, Optima Batteries, Inc., Hauser Chemical, Coors ACX, Ceramics and Brewing, Monfort Beef, Rocky Mountain Cancer Center, Keebler, COBE Labs and projects for Jefferson County Schools.

Piper Electric generously contributes both time and money to a variety of organizations in and around Jefferson County. Local involvement includes The Arvada Center for the Arts & Humanities, The Arvada Food Bank, Career Awareness Programs in area schools, Women in Crisis/Family Tree and the Children's Advocacy Center. Outside of Jefferson County, Piper helps to support the Leukemia Society of America, the Bannock Shelter, Boulder County Safe House, and the Inner City Health Center, just to name a few.

The mission of Piper Electric is to be the best provider of advanced technological support to commerce and industry through innovative engineering, construction and service. As a result, Piper Electric Company remains a leader in its industry not only in Colorado, but throughout the United States. That's Piper Electric—Your Power Performance Team.

Above: Electrical and pneumatic controls at Bolder Technologies Corporation.

Below: Piper technicians do final checkout of computerized controls at Bolder Technologies Corporation in Golden, Colorado.
PHOTOS COURTESY OF PHILIP WEGENER KANTOR.

HAZEN RESEARCH, INC.

Above: Analytical laboratory and administration building.

Below: Acamite mineral as seen through a high-powered microscope.

Hazen Research, Inc. is an employee-owned industrial research and development firm located in Golden. The company was founded in 1961 by H.L. Hazen, a highly respected metallurgical consultant, and a small group of metallurgists with strong backgrounds in research and process development for the mining and chemical industries. Over the years, Hazen has grown to its present size of 170 employees, with 15 buildings containing an extensive inventory of laboratory and pilot plant equipment. The highly experienced and competent staff members at Hazen work with state-of-the-art laboratory and pilot plant facilities that support their ability to apply the most appropriate technology to the industrial, commercial and environmental concerns of their clients. Combined, they serve clients from all over the world on projects ranging from bench-scale experiments and analyses to multimillion-dollar continuous pilot plants.

The company's original focus was on mining and metallurgical activities, and it has a worldwide reputation for excellence in the application of mineralogy to the resolution of processing problems. However, it soon became evident that the skills and knowledge needed to recover metals from ore were equally applicable to removing toxic substances from waste materials of environmental concerns. As a result, Hazen has expanded its range of services to include the environmental and energy industries. The expertise of its employees allows the company to provide its clients with practical resolutions for industrial waste problems, including not only the best technological processes but also the knowledge of the relevant regulatory and licensing requirements.

Hazen is the largest firm in the United States specializing in metallurgical and chemical research for industry and has completed over 9,000 projects for nearly 800 industrial clients. The company has completed hundreds of gold projects and has been associated with most of the refractory gold research that provided basic metallurgical design criteria for plants now operating in Nevada and elsewhere. In addition to its research and development activities, Hazen provides preliminary layouts and cost estimates for small-scale industrial chemical plants and mineral-treatment facilities. Its ability to fabricate and

operate small demonstration plants on and off site has required a parallel development of sophisticated data acquisition and computer modeling methods. Continuous development has resulted in newly installed facilities to handle complex high-pressure leach and solvent extraction processes for treating such ores as nickel laterites and gold-bearing sulfides. The company completed over $12 million worth of research and development for industrial clients in fiscal 1997.

The product of Hazen is knowledge; the knowledge needed by clients to make use of the best processes in an increasingly competitive world. The strength of the company is its employees' ability to understand and provide service in the entire spectrum of any project activity. There are few places in North America where an industry can obtain mineral, chemical, thermal and physical process engineering services in a single location. This fact allows Hazen to provide its customers with convenience and time savings.

One key to Hazen's overall project success is communication. Project managers at Hazen work directly with their clients and stay in touch with them to ensure expectations and needs are met throughout each program. This is achieved through regular meetings with clients to jointly examine the project data as it becomes available and implementing program changes, when necessary. It is also achieved through the collective teamwork of what is believed to be the finest broad-based technical staff of its kind in the world—a staff that includes chemists, metallurgists, chemical and metallurgical engineers, mineralogists, trained technicians and

craftsmen along with capable administrative and support personnel.

Hazen is not a business that is run from the top: everyone on the staff must have an entrepreneurial spirit to flourish in this environment. Averaging one new project per day, the research staff members have the very best analytical instruments, laboratory research apparatus and pilot plants at their disposal. They are responsible for seeking out clients, understanding their needs and finding innovative methods for delivering the required services even when conventional technology does not apply.

Hazen has been granted permits by the EPA and the Colorado Department of Public Health and Environment for RCRA, TSCA and RD&D treatability studies. It also holds a license from the Nuclear Regulatory Commission to conduct studies on material containing radioactive constituents.

Currently in a period of high growth, Hazen Research, Inc. remains dedicated to the principle of quality performance, which means the company intends to meet and exceed each client's expectations while ensuring a safe environment for its employees and the community at large.

Above: X-ray diffraction.

Below: Solvent extraction separation of metals.

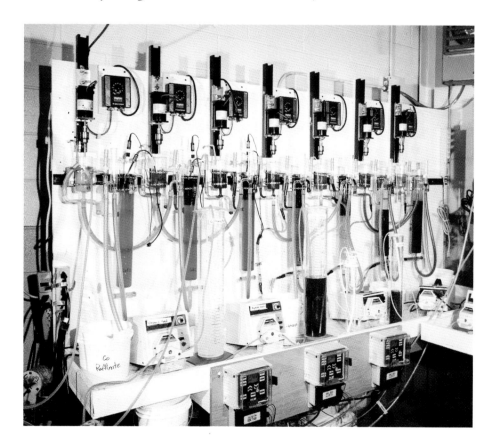

EVERGREEN MEMORIAL PARK

Above: An old-fashion funeral procession.

Below: Garden of the Pioneers.

Evergreen Memorial Park has a diverse and complementary function—cemetery (human and pet), funeral home, crematory, wedding chapel, living museum and wildlife preserve. Perhaps more importantly, its existence speaks to the significance of our heritage and the value of preserving an important imprint of the Old West while still meeting contemporary needs of our region's growing population.

Located south of Evergreen at 26624 North Turkey Creek Road, the property was originally purchased as a ranch in 1965 by Ron and Carol Lewis. The Lewises have kept the 100-acre site as a tribute to the pioneers of Evergreen and the Old West. Most of the land is used as private animal reserve with resident coyotes, owls, horses, elk, buffalo, deer, ducks, geese, swans, muskrats and one particularly faithful heron.

The pride of the preserve is the Lewis' buffalo herd. These animals have a direct blood-line to the original Great Plains bison—the American "buffalo".

Spring is a delightful time at Evergreen Memorial Park as onlookers abound to view the young animals just born. A stop at the Park takes visitors back in time as they watch the great animals they would have seen more than 100 years ago.

As well as protecting wildlife, the Lewises strive to preserve the pioneer heritage of the Old West at Evergreen Memorial Park. They are antique buffs and have collected historically important artifacts of the Old West for many years. The Lodge and property display native American arrowheads, stone implements and tools from local farming, mining and timbering industries of the past. Wagons, tractors and plows, discovered on neighboring ranches, serve as reminders of the era when Evergreen was once considered the potato capital of Colorado.

The Memorial Park's Garden of the Pioneers has stone and timber cabins serving as its centerpiece, creating a sentimental tribute to the early pioneers. Edward Steele, a mule skinner in his youth, was buried on this memorial site in 1980. In keeping with the wishes of the Steele family, Mr. Steele was buried in a simple, old-fashioned manner. With a horse-drawn hearse and a pine coffin decorated with a hand-carved wooden gun on the lid, history was relived the day he was laid to rest. On that cold, blustery January morning, Edward Steele and his procession of family members and life-long friends made their way through the

Garden. So significant was Mr. Steeles' passing in its historical simplicity that a Channel 9 TV news team respectfully documented the event. Pine coffins and the same antique hearse that carried Mr. Steele are still used today in many funeral services at the Park.

Jessie Pierre, the Queen of Morrison Centennial Days and the oldest continuous resident of Jefferson County, is also buried in the Park as are others whose hearts have returned to the mountains.

As an alternative to the urban cemetery, Evergreen Memorial Park provides a peaceful mountain valley setting in which to celebrate life. Reflecting the simplicity of our western heritage, burial options range from a traditional graveside ceremony to the burial or scattering of remains. The dedication of the Lewis family and staff to helping individuals through the grieving process results in meaningful and memorable ceremonies. Their unconditional giving has touched the lives of many people over the years and helped individuals rebuild relationships. Often at their suggestion, friends and family members are encouraged to share the uniqueness of the life being honored through a wide range of personal expression—a medley of favorite songs, items from a personal collection, a photographic journey, the showing of an artist's work. Special aspects such as these and many others have been intimately woven into ceremonies as symbols that link the past to the present.

Evergreen Memorial Park is non-denominational. However, its services are Christian. Ron and Carol Lewis take great joy in offering the use of their rustic Great Room Chapel or outdoor meadow area for sanctifying marriage vows, baptisms, graduations, anniversaries, or saying good-bye to someone close. Regardless of the occasion, the Lewises are pleased to help make a special event of any kind both sacred and healing.

The Great Room Chapel at Evergreen Memorial Park comfortably seats fifty to sixty people, and thirty more people can be seated in the adjacent solar area. Large and small events are welcome on the outdoor grounds, with all areas handicap accessible.

A recent addition to Evergreen Memorial Park is a 110 year-old pioneer barn from the Sanger Ranch, now developed as The Homestead. It is being restored and expanded as a new chapel, mausoleum and columbarium and will seat over 200 people. This barn serves as yet another unique reminder of our fading western history.

The Park has an endowment care fund to guarantee its future maintenance. It is licensed to sell pre-need and has a trust established to care for the moneys of those sales.

Whether celebrating in an elaborate or simple fashion, Evergreen Memorial Park is a unique place to rekindle the spirit that abounds in our western heritage, especially for those who feel most at home in the mountains.

Above: Ron Lewis with Doorfus, a prized bull elk.

Below: A picturesque wedding on the grounds.

GEOMATION, INC.

Below: Revelstoke Dam, British Columbia, Canada. Geomation data acquisition and control equipment is used for safety and performance monitoring of the dam.

PHOTO COURTESY OF BC HYDRO.

A small electronic manufacturer in Golden is making a global name for itself by providing safety-monitoring systems for literally millions of people worldwide. Over the last decade, Geomation, Inc. has provided safety and performance monitoring systems for some of the world's largest civil engineering projects, including Ertan Dam and the Tian Huang Ping Pumped Storage Projects in China, the Boston Central Artery Project and the Eastside Reservoir water supply project in southern California. Geomation equipment is being used at hundreds of other locations throughout the United States and Canada, as well as in China, Latin America, India and the Caribbean. In any given year, 40% to 50% of the revenues for this local company come from its international clientele. In 1993, Geomation, Inc. was the recipient of the Governor's Award for Excellence in Exporting.

In the 1970s, Teton, Canyon Lake and Buffalo Creek Dams failed catastrophically, sending shock waves through water resource organizations and the civil engineering profession. Regulators scrambled to explain the failures because they didn't match up with the otherwise proud history of dam safety in the United States. The thousands of aging dams whose safety had been taken for granted were now posing political, economic and possible national security threats. As a result, the instrumentation and monitoring practices on all high hazard dams came under review by both federal and state agencies. The U.S. Bureau of Reclamation and the U.S. Army Corps of Engineers, federal operators of the largest high hazard dams, initiated programs to review the safety of existing dams and foster the development of instrumentation and monitoring technology that could lead to more effective and timely observations of the safety and long-term performance of dams.

These renewed safety efforts at the federal level were the impetus for John Klebba, company founder and President, to respond to what he perceived as a new market opportunity—to implement real-time data acquisition systems for dam safety instrumentation.

Geomation, Inc. was founded in 1982. For the first two years, efforts were directed to market discovery, product research and system design. By late 1984, a comprehensive product plan was developed to address the general class of battery-operated, wireless- and cable-networked systems for field data acquisition and control. Geomation's initial focus was on the dam safety monitoring requirements identified by the U.S. Bureau of Reclamation, the U.S. Army Corps of Engineers and several of the large hydropower utility companies in the United States and Canada. This research and development activity culminated with the introduction in 1986 of the Geomation System 2300, an innovative data acquisition and control system employing a node-driven architecture, which is unique in the industry for battery-powered instrumentation systems.

According to Dr. Ken Hultman, Vice President of Engineering, this node-driven (or peer-to-peer) system architecture allows intelligent remote Measurement and Control Units (MCUs) to operate with very low power consumption without compromising other important performance objectives. Garry Southard, Vice President of Sales and Marketing, observes that a large part of the

success of the Geomation system is due to flexibility provided by the system design. These systems can be applied to a variety of field automation requirements as totally standard products, due to extensive user-programmability for both networking and instrumentation functions.

Networking strategies supported by Geomation MCUs include radio, wireline, fiber-optics, microwave, satellite and both public and private switched telecom networks. MCUs support arbitrary user-programmable message routing, media bridging and automatic switched-network access, all with error-checked message transactions from source to destination. The operating interface software, GEONET™ Suite, provides new capabilities for linking field-distributed instrumentation with enterprise information management systems using open-architecture 32-bit database technology. Field data can be accessed through the Internet or intranets, providing a uniform communications infrastructure for global data transport. GEONET Suite is fully Y2K compliant and runs on Windows 95, Windows 98 and Windows NT systems.

Today, Geomation Inc. manufactures and markets an integrated family of standard hardware and software products providing "total system solutions" for a variety of field data collection and other automation applications. With the inherent flexibility in both system architecture and product designs, Geomation's third generation products are used extensively for large civil construction (dams and tunnels), water resource facilities (wastewater collection and water distribution), and environmental monitoring applications. Geomation's primary customers continue to be domestic and foreign governmental agencies, hydro-power, water supply and water reclamation utilities, large industrial concerns, and large engineering and construction firms engaged in water resources and transportation development projects. Products are either sold directly to end-users, through engineering consulting firms, or through manufacturers of measurement devices used in large civil construction.

Geomation's continuing vision is to provide products to overcome the traditional barriers that have denied the benefits of automation in remote and harsh environments. This is the vision which inspired the name of Geomation, Inc. over fifteen years ago, and the vision which will provide economic opportunities for growth well into the next millennium.

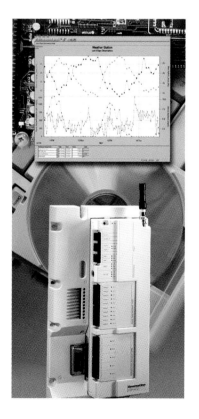

HOLIDAY INN LAKEWOOD/ DENVER

Right: Holiday Inn Lakewood, located at Hampden Avenue and Wadsworth Boulevard, provides all the attention and amenities guests deserve.

Below: The newly renovated lobby reflects the sophisticated comfort guests can expect to find throughout their stay.

The Holiday Inn experience begins the moment guests walk into the spacious and inviting lobby. The Inn's personalized approach to service makes every guest feel special by providing all the attention and amenities they deserve and expect to find from a fine hotel.

Voted as Lakewood's Finest Full-Service Value among the local business community, the Holiday Inn Lakewood is the only full-service hotel in southwest Denver. Ideally located at Hampden Avenue and Wadsworth Boulevard, the Inn is adjacent to Academy Park Place and just minutes from the Denver Federal Center. Its location provides easy access to the excitement of downtown Denver, surrounding Jefferson County communities and the beauty of the Rocky Mountains. Whether guests stay at the Holiday Inn Lakewood for business or pleasure, they will find the accommodations convenient and the experience enjoyable.

The Inn's own Winner's Circle Restaurant offers superb American Cuisine that is sure to please the most discriminating palate. It is open daily and offers room service for guests who choose to dine in or in the comfort of their own room. In addition, the Equestrian Lounge is the perfect spot for relaxing with friends or colleagues for a quiet chat and refreshments. The Lounge offers complimentary hors d'oeuvres and drink specials from 5:00 to 7:00 p.m. every weekday.

In 1998, Holiday Inn Lakewood underwent $1,000,000 in renovation and enhancements. Each of the Inn's 190 upscale guest rooms and suites offers sophisticated comfort and a host of special amenities. Rooms are beautifully appointed with elegant cherry wood furnishings, a king bed or two oversized double beds, and boasts a comfortable seating and writing area. The added touches that lend elegant comfort for travelers include: in-room coffee maker and hair dryer, in-room iron and ironing board, oversized bathroom, cable television, pay-per-view movies and a data port. And for added convenience, there is a gift shop, game room and guest laundry facility on the premises.

Unequaled anywhere in southwest Denver, Holiday Inn Lakewood

offers 5,000 square feet of flexible meeting, banquet and conference space. Whether it's a small board meeting for six or a formal affair for 250, Holiday Inn Lakewood will cater to every requirement with style and ease. The Inn's professional catering staff helps to round out the perfect setting and ambiance to ensure a truly rewarding experience.

Recreation makes a visit to Holiday Inn Lakewood complete. Guests can re-energize in the Inn's guest-only exercise facility or use a complimentary pass to an acclaimed athletic club nearby. After a workout, they can take a refreshing dip in the seasonal outdoor swimming pool or ease into the steaming whirlpool or sauna.

Most of all, Holiday Inn Lakewood is renowned for its professional and personalized approach to service. The Inn is rated in the top 10% of all Holiday Inns and has twice been awarded the Quality Excellence award through Bass Hotels for consistently providing exceptional customer service. The Inn has also been rated the number one full-service Holiday Inn in the Denver metropolitan area for superior service over the past several years. Its more than sixty-five full-time employees allow the Inn to offer the utmost in customer service and hospitality. All of these aspects contribute to why guests find the Inn's warmth and accommodations unmatched by other locations.

Holiday Inn Lakewood is owned and operated by Larken Management Company which owns and operates thirteen other hotels throughout the United States, including other Holiday Inns, Sheraton Hotels and the Hilton in Bloomington, Minnesota. Ed Sellers, CHA, has been the General Manager of Holiday Inn Lakewood for over ten years. Known throughout the community for his involvement in the West Chamber and Golden Chamber of Commerce, and as a long-time resident of Colorado, Mr. Sellers had once owned the Old Heidelberg Inn in Golden which was renowned for its fine German Cuisine.

The Holiday Inn Lakewood is a proud supporter and sponsor of the Give Kids the World Foundation. With more than 70% of terminally ill children requesting a trip to Central Florida and the Walt Disney World Resort, Give Kids the World works with more than 350 wish-granting foundations, hospitals and hospices around the world to fulfill the wish of these children to meet Mickey Mouse. Started in 1989 with the financial support of Holiday Inns, Give Kids the World has served over 31,000 families from all fifty states and forty-five countries. All of this started with the vision of one man, Henri Landwirth. Mr. Landwirth, a childhood Holocaust survivor, has vowed no child would be turned away from Give Kids the World, and no child ever has.

Holiday Inn Lakewood is committed to making every guest's stay as relaxing and rewarding as can be imagined. Make Holiday Inn Lakewood your next stop while in the area and notice the difference.

Banquet facilities and catering options create the perfect ambiance for up to 250 guests.

GREEN GABLES COUNTRY CLUB

Above: The grand estate at Green Gables Club House.

Below: Players putting on the ninth hole.

The moment you drive through the magnificent wrought-iron entry gate of Green Gables Country Club, the pressures of work begin to fade away. Here, in a stunning park-like setting that boasts a full complement of sporting activities, the word "leisure" takes on a new meaning. Whether you are a golf enthusiast, a tennis buff, an avid swimmer, or simply someone who appreciates the idea of having a home away from home, Green Gables is a country club unmatched by others.

Prior to its purchase in 1928 by Green Gables Realty, the grounds belonged to Cripple Creek silver baron Verner Reed. As an isolated patch of manicured green, the estate ran along a dusty Morrison Road which served as the gateway to the silver camps of the Colorado Rockies.

Twenty-four influential members of the Denver Jewish community comprised Green Gables Realty. Although they did not announce their plans for the country club the first year, they quickly began their development. The original colonial manor was converted into the clubhouse, and by 1931, the club had finished a nine-hole golf course. WW II interrupted completion of the course, but it was finalized shortly thereafter.

By the 1950s, Green Gables Country Club boasted one of the finest eighteen-hole golf courses in Denver. The course was so popular that in September of 1955, President Dwight D. Eisenhower stopped to play golf and attend a dinner in his honor. Photos of this historic event still line the walls in the main entrance of the clubhouse.

Today, Green Gables remains an "isolated patch of manicured green" tucked along Jewell Avenue and Wadsworth Boulevard. Novices and pros alike enjoy playing the championship course as they take in the constant views of the glorious snow-capped Rocky Mountains.

Green Gables Country Club has served Denver residents and their families for generations. Toddlers have learned to swim and junior members have celebrated their passage into adulthood. The club will continue to be a place where milestones are achieved and families relax but with an energy that is shifting with the times.

Over the past few years, the sport of golf has gained heightened appeal among the younger members of Green Gables. Of the club's 500 members, nearly 400 use the greens, bringing an extraordinarily high level of excitement and energy to the grounds in summer. The club has thriving men's and women's golf associations which offer something for everyone; twilight golfing events for couples, a nine-hole association for women new to the sport and an eighteen-hole association for the more seasoned golfer, along with clinics throughout the season for enthusiasts at all levels.

A strong summer youth program draws children of all ages to Green Gables. Members can enroll their five to ten year-old children or grandchildren in a day-summer camp series that features golf, tennis, swimming, arts and crafts, nature hikes, basketball and much more. Junior tennis and golf clinics are offered twice each season for youngsters ages seven to seventeen. Both clinics cover all facets of the games and offer participants the chance to practice and improve their skills under the guidance of highly qualified instructors.

A highlight of the summer is the barbecue held in celebration of July 4, complete with fireworks and carnival. Close to 900 people attend each year, making this one of the most spectacular events hosted at Green Gables for the entire membership.

Other seasonal events include theme dinners, biweekly summer barbecues, dance lessons during the winter, computer classes and holiday gatherings.

The club takes special pride in hosting weddings, parties and private meetings throughout the year with banquet facilities for up to 450 people. With culinary facilities that are second to none, Green Gables offers traditional Jewish delicacies at their Sunday brunches, Passover Seders and monthly Shabbat dinners. The club's chef and his staff are noted for producing an array of gourmet delights.

The outdoor terrace Grill offers casual dining with a light fare of deli sandwiches, while the elegant Renaissance Room offers a more traditional menu and ensures a highly memorable dining experience for patrons.

Green Gables Country Club is a tradition for many members. But it is a tradition that is changing with the times. Long-time and new members will find amenities to meet their needs at any time throughout the year; for it is the members who create the appeal and make Green Gables Country Club a home away from home.

Top, left: Fifth hole fairway looking west.

Top, right: Banquet hall prepared for one of the many summer galas at Green Gables Country Club.

Below: Players starting a round at the first tee.

DEVELOPMENTAL DISABILITIES RESOURCE CENTER

Above: Larry Austin at Safe T Gard.

Below: Art Hogling, Executive Director, Developmental Disabilities Resource Center.

THE DEVELOPMENTAL DISABILITIES RESOURCE CENTER: A VITAL RESOURCE FOR THE PEOPLE OF JEFFERSON COUNTY

The Developmental Disabilities Resource Center (DDRC) is a nonprofit agency which provides services to over 1,400 families and individuals with developmental disabilities living in Jefferson, Clear Creek, Gilpin and Summit counties.

"Our mission — to promote quality, dignity and choice for people with developmental disabilities and their families — is evident in our infant, adolescent, adult, family and recreational programs," said DDRC Executive Director Art Hogling, Ph.D.

DDRC has had a long-standing commitment to provide positive, life enhancing choices for individuals and their families through strong and vital programs. "First and foremost, the Developmental Disabilities Resource Center is about community services," said Hogling.

"It is our goal to make certain that people and families who need our programs are well aware of them and can benefit from them and, equally important, if we cannot help, then we are willing to help find options," continued Hogling.

DDRC, formerly the Jefferson County Community Center for Developmental Disabilities, has been providing community services since 1964. Programs are supported by private contributions, grants, federal, state and local funds. DDRC operates three schools, vocational centers and a wide range of residential options.

Honored by President Bush as Colorado's first recipient of a "Thousand Points of Light" award, DDRC works with over 100 local businesses to provide jobs, assist people living in local neighborhoods who need help on a day-to-day basis, and provides ongoing education and training for developmentally disabled children and their families.

EMPLOYMENT SERVICES

Holding down a job is a large part of achieving independence. DDRC, through partnerships with business and industry, gives individuals a variety of employment choices not available in traditional programs.

DDRC provides employment for approximately 200 individuals in the community and 125 at the Bruno Vocational Training Center. DDRC offers a variety of employment options including manufacturing, packaging, retail, groundskeeping, janitorial services and food service.

For instance, Larry Austin is one of many successful participants in DDRC's Employment Services. Five years ago, Austin went to work for Safe T Gard, a Jefferson County based manufacturer of sporting equipment. Through his experience, Larry has been able to save money, take vacations and gain a greater sense of independence.

Additionally, the benefits to employers are many. They include potential tax credits, motivated employees, employee longevity, strong safety records and savings in recruitment and training.

"Safe T Gard has gained valuable and reliable employees through our partnership with DDRC," said Safe T Gard CEO Scott Jacobs. "The program is not only worthwhile for employees, but also a solid investment in our workforce."

When working with local employers, DDRC screens applicants and assists with job analysis, job modifications and on-the-job training. Ongoing consultation is available to both the employer and the employee.

"We have a solid track record of helping people maintain jobs for a long period of time," said Diana Holland, Employment and Training Services Director. "But our number one goal remains, finding jobs people like while meeting employers' needs."

Top, left: Joy Jones at Bruno Vocational Center working for Jolly Rancher.

Top, right: Cliff Stroup at Conoco.

Below: Becky Kennedy at King Soopers.

EMICH WEST

Step through the doors at either the Oldsmobile/GMC Truck/Subaru store or the Jeep/Eagle store on West Colfax in Golden and you will quickly understand why Emich Automotive is the "name you've come to trust" in the auto industry. Whether you are talking with a sales representative or the store manager, you will easily sense that your car buying experience will be positive no matter what preconception you had walking onto the property. Your questions will be answered, your concerns will be heard and you will walk away a satisfied customer, even if the exact car you want is not on one of these two lots. These two Jefferson County auto stores are very different in terms of products and clientele but very much the same in what they offer: quality service and a high level of expertise.

Started in 1975 as Emich Oldsmobile on Sixth Avenue and Simms in Lakewood, Fred Emich has upheld a family tradition started years ago by his grandfather. That tradition is great customer service.

Emich Automotive has grown tremendously because of its loyal customer base which has developed over the years. Fred Emich learned from his father and grandfather that the only way to stay in business was to take care of your clientele before, during and after they purchase their cars. That means having a "conversation" about cars with a customer, not "talking to" a customer about cars. It also means listening to the customer, being the

primary point of contact and following up after the sale. Each sales representative stays in touch with his customers through phone calls and letters to ensure their satisfaction and to remind the customers that Emich is there when they need them. Establishing long-term relationships is the ultimate goal. To that end, Emich Automotive employees live by the belief that when they sell someone a car, they sell the entire family a car, and it is quite likely they will eventually sell another car to that family.

The Emich Oldsmobile West store is the original store at a new location and a model of how customers are treated at all other Emich locations. Customers are always met with courtesy and consistency; two important aspects of Fred Emich's operating philosophy.

Because Emich treats its employees like family, employees in turn treat their customers like family—with fairness, respect, courtesy, and on a personal level. "It's the people who make the difference," say Dave Dunn and Jeff O'Leary, general managers of the Oldsmobile/GMC Truck/Subaru and Jeep/Eagle stores respectively. Jeff has been with Emich for over twenty-one years; Dave for over eight years.

Each employee brings an incredible amount of experience to the car-buying process at the Emich stores. It is not unusual to find employees who have been with Fred from the start and others with over thirty years of experience in the auto industry. Employing over 200 people between the two stores, Oldsmobile/GMC Truck/Subaru and Jeep/Eagle have seventy-two employees who have been with the company since opening at their present location and more than sixty employees with over ten years of service.

Emich Jeep/Eagle.

Those more recent employees who join the close-knit Emich team and are dedicated to providing quality service are polished and given the training they need to make a difference to the customers who walk through their doors. The company prides itself on investing in its employees by providing extensive and on-going training, whether product training for its sales force or service training for its mechanics.

Today, eight dealerships and thirteen franchises strong, Emich Automotive is a leader in its industry both regionally and nationally. Since the two Jefferson County stores consolidated lots in August of 1990, Jeff O'Leary's Jeep/Eagle store has been honored annually as the number one producing Jeep store in a seven state region. Both the Jeep/Eagle and GMC Truck stores have received the National Five Star Award of Excellence, the highest award bestowed in the industry.

Both the Oldsmobile/GMC Truck/Subaru store and the Jeep/Eagle store belong to the West Chamber and support many youth oriented programs throughout the county. Together, they sponsor an annual golf tournament to benefit the D.A.R.E. program, contribute to Red Rocks Community College and participate in providing numerous scholarship awards to Jefferson County students.

What do Dave Dunn and Jeff O'Leary find to be the greatest challenges in today's automobile industry? Increased competition, better quality vehicles and customers who are more demanding. With customers walking through the doors better informed about cars and knowing how to find answers to their questions, sales representatives must listen more carefully to what their customers want and deliver products and services in a manner that meets the customer's needs. But that's not a problem. It's what Emich does best.

A strong, stable business working in a strong, stable community. Emich West. The name you've come to trust.

*Emich Oldsmobile/
GMC Truck/Subaru.*

JEFFERSON CENTER FOR MENTAL HEALTH

Right: Jefferson Center's programs are provided for all age groups. From its Counselors in the Schools Program to its Nursing Home Treatment Programs, JCMH provides care for the entire community.

Below: Under the leadership of President and Chief Executive Officer Harriet Hall, Ph.D., Jefferson Center for Mental Health has grown into one of Colorado's largest and most respected community mental health centers.

Less than fifty years ago, people with mental illness were shunned and locked away. The stigma of mental illness kept individuals isolated and their families living with a "secret" that they were afraid to share.

When Jefferson Center for Mental Health (JCMH) started serving the community, it began with the dream of getting people with mental illness and children with severe emotional problems out of the institutions where they were living and into the community where they could be productive citizens. The Center provided services in a small one-room clinic in the basement of the Jefferson County Courthouse with little funding and three part-time employees.

Through forty years of service, Jefferson Center's dream has become a reality. People with mental illness are a part of the community—working, raising families and leading fulfilling lives. Every year, 6,000 children, teens, adults and older adults receive services from Jefferson Center in thirty locations across its three county region.

Jefferson Center for Mental Health is a private, non-profit community mental health center, serving residents of Jefferson, Gilpin and Clear Creek Counties. Celebrating forty years of service, JCMH now provides a wide range of innovative programs that help to improve the lives of individuals and families impacted by mental illness.

The Center focuses on assisting people with serious and persistent mental health issues by employing the most appropriate healthcare alternatives available. Depending on the nature of the diagnosis, that may mean providing minimally restric-

tive options such as counseling, community education and prevention efforts or more intensive services such as in-home treatment, day treatment and vocational programs.

Jefferson Center's care network continues to grow as needs increase. Currently, an estimated one in four families is impacted by some type of mental illness, and mental healthcare and substance abuse treatment account for at least 10% of employee health costs. But figures also show that appropriate and timely treatment of severe mental health disorders can result in a 10% decrease in use and cost of medical services making Jefferson Center's services critical to the community.

To increase access to services, Jefferson Center has partnered with other community-based programs, meaning that Jefferson County is now served by programs such as the Jefferson County Juvenile Assessment Center, Family Adolescent Crisis Team (F.A.C.T.), School Based Services, Family Centers, Master Planning and the Mountain Family Project. In addition to the Center's

network of external providers, nearly 300 individuals make up the Center's staff including psychiatrists, psychologists, psychiatric nurses, licensed clinical social workers, case managers and vocational counselors. Not only do these staff members work hard to attend to the day-to-day needs of their clients, they extend their commitment to community and healthcare by collectively serving on most major human services boards and task forces throughout the community.

Support for mental health services has come through a variety of funding sources including state and federal funding. In 1997, the Jefferson Center Board of Directors realized that unless new sources of support were found, many of the services that were critical to people with mental illness and to children and their families would be in danger of being reduced or cut completely.

In order to meet Jefferson Center's commitment to the people of the community, new resources needed to be developed. The Board of Directors responded by establishing a Foundation to build long-term support from individuals, businesses, foundations and other community organizations. Jefferson

Center's Foundation gives people an opportunity to support the programs that are important to them—to help Jefferson Center develop the resources that give people with mental illness new hope and reach children and their families before their problems become overwhelming.

The Foundation seeks financial support for Jefferson Center, but the Foundation also provides support to other organizations whose activities or projects are consistent with the mission and values of the Foundation and the Center. By educating the community about mental illness, the Foundation builds support in the community for mental health programs. It provides a focus for giving by donors who want to ensure that mental health services will be available to meet future needs and who support innovative programs to meet current needs. At the same time, those donors can receive important tax benefits.

Jefferson Center for Mental Health and the Foundation are a team that believes children need opportunities to grow to their full potential, that people with mental illness can lead fulfilling lives, that older adults have the right to enjoy their later years free of debilitating, life-threatening depression and that every person with mental illness can find the help they need and joy in life again.

Together We Can Make a Difference! Jefferson Center for Mental Health.

Left: Jefferson Center's Access Center provides a single-entry point for consumer information, referral, assessment and advocacy services. It also acts as the coordination point for emergency mental health services for the three county area.

Below: Jefferson Center's Access Center and administrative office is located at 5265 Vance Street in Arvada. JCMH provides services in over thirty locations throughout Jefferson, Gilpin and Clear Creek Counties.

GEORGE T. SANDERS COMPANY

Above: George T. Sanders Company officers from left: Matt Sanders, Michael Raisch, Thomas Tooley, Gary Sanders, Corporate Council Robert Loeb. Mrs. Beverly Sanders not pictured.

Below: One of forty-six trucks preparing for delivery.

George T. Sanders Company opened its doors in the spring of 1950 as a small company supplying sheet metal and other industry materials to heating contractors in Denver. Started by George T. Sanders and his wife, Pauline, the company quickly outgrew its original location at 1111 Stout Street in downtown Denver. After much needed expansion and several locations later, George T. Sanders Company makes its home at 10201 West 49th Avenue in Wheat Ridge and operates nine additional branches throughout Colorado. The company is one of the largest and most successful independent plumbing and radiant heating supply houses in the state as well as one of the largest suppliers of copper pipe to plumbing and mechanical contractors.

The strength of George T. Sanders Company is its family's history and involvement. After building the business with her husband, Mrs. Pauline Sanders served as interim president after Mr. George Sanders passed away in 1972 and until management was turned over to their two sons, Norman and Gary. The brothers shared management responsibilities for nearly twenty years before Gary, the younger of George and Pauline's two sons, purchased the company in 1990. Today, the company is owned and managed by Gary and has a staff of nearly fifty employees at the Wheat Ridge location alone.

Over the years, inevitable changes have occurred for George T. Sanders Company — changes in location, management and staff, even the type of inventory the company stocks. However, one thing that has not changed is the company's commitment to supplying its customers with quality products and doing so with a high level of professional service.

The guiding principles upon which George T. Sanders Company was built and continues to operate to achieve success include teamwork, a commitment to providing quality products and service, and a creative approach to solving problems. By stressing these principles, the company has attracted and retained many capable employees along with a solid and satisfied customer base. Employees know they will be treated fairly and with respect as professionals in their industry. The company's management expects a great deal from those they hire, and in return, can be counted on to provide a great deal of support and a high level of investment to help its employees pursue industry opportunities that enhance their personal development.

Customers as well have proven that they recognize the value George T. Sanders

Company adds to the wholesale plumbing and supply industry. Customers have demonstrated their loyalty by supporting and rewarding the company with continued growth and profitability over many years. In return, the company's belief and dedication to its customers has allowed them to continue to provide great customer service which has led to successful growth.

Gary Sanders and his staff believe in providing quality service not just during the sale but before and after as well. This means educating customers and providing service on the front end in addition to delivering materials and supplies, when necessary, to customers in the field. With nearly 100 employees and a fleet of forty-six vehicles among the Wheat Ridge and statewide branches in Quebec, Silverthorne, Basalt, Montrose, Ft. Collins, Highlands Ranch, Louisville and Colorado Springs, George T. Sanders Company successfully competes with national companies in providing wholesale plumbing equipment.

Each branch employs approximately five to ten people who are responsible for management, service and delivery to regional customers. The manager of each location is given full responsibility for his store and allowed to make primary decisions for how the branch is operated. Since the operating and customer needs within each location vary, placing the decision-making in the hands of the branch managers encourages full leadership and commitment to the stores' success and profitability.

Although George T. Sanders Company is a small and closely held firm, it is a member of

C. L. Watt, Inc. of which Gary Sanders currently serves as president. C. L. Watt is a buying cooperative within the plumbing industry that brings power to the negotiation process with vendors and allows discounts to its nearly forty-five independent company membership. The organization is an excellent resource for technical and business concerns common among these industry companies throughout the United States.

Other local and national organizations to which George T. Sanders Company holds membership and offers support include the American Supply Association, the Wholesale Distribution Association, the National Association of Credit Management, and the Financial Executive Institute. In addition, the company contributes to Light for Life Foundation of America, a non-profit youth organization.

In a rapidly changing industry, George T. Sanders Company has changed with the times. It has expanded and updated its systems to promote greater efficiency within distribution channels and will continue to do so as the future unfolds. But despite the myriad rapid changes, customers of George T. Sanders Company can rest assured they will receive quality products and service well into the next millennium.

Above: Central warehouse facility in Wheat Ridge.

Below: Partial copper piping inventory used to supply plumbing and mechanical contractors.

ROCKY MOUNTAIN REMEDIATION SERVICES, L.L.C.

In 1994, Colorado saw a new firm come into existence to support the environmental cleanup activities at the Rocky Flats Environmental Technology Site and other sites throughout Colorado and the United States. Rocky Mountain Remediation Services, L.L.C. (RMRS), the strategic integration of Morrison Knudsen Corporation and BNFL, Inc., is a leader in radioactive and hazardous materials management, environmental remediation, waste management, and decontamination and decommissioning (D&D).

RMRS' Colorado history began in 1995 with the cleanup of Rocky Flats. As part of the Kaiser-Hill team of contractors, RMRS provides environmental restoration, waste management, and D&D services for the site. With the focus of closing Rocky Flats by 2006, RMRS offers Kaiser-Hill, the government and the local Denver area communities the proven experience to successfully move waste off the site, clean up contaminated areas, and decommission and demolish the buildings; improving the area's skyline.

To its credit, RMRS has surpassed its previous years' accomplishments by continuously shipping more and more waste offsite. It

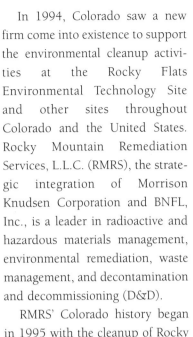

RMRS performs waste management, environmental restoration, and decommissioning.

continues to remove surplus facilities after decommissioning them and has demolished more than twenty-five facilities between 1995 and 1998. In 1997, RMRS' safety record was the best in the Department of Energy Complex, and it continues to improve.

RMRS is committed to obtaining additional work within Colorado and elsewhere in the United States, creating employment opportunities for its employees upon the closure of Rocky Flats.

When RMRS formed in 1994, the company brought with it the expertise and knowledge of its parent companies through the strategic transfer of fifty core personnel. The remaining staff members, which in 1998 was close to 275, were hired from the existing Rocky Flats workforce, ensuring an infusion of the expertise and knowledge of the site before operations ceased. With this combined expertise, RMRS offers its clients an experienced workforce with a thorough understanding of the regulations and requirements associated with cleaning up some of the most hazardous and radioactively contaminated sites in Colorado and the United States.

With headquarters in Golden, RMRS also supports the cleanup of many of the contaminated sites along Clear Creek Canyon. With a technology designed by its employees, the local communities are beginning to see the contaminated soils along Clear Creek being removed and cleaned for future use. This technology is called Envirobond™/Envirobric™ and has the following advantages:

- Bonds with the strength of glass at room temperature.
- Provides 30% to 50% volume reduction
- Uses high throughput, cost effective, field-proven equipment.

This process uses a non-hazardous chemical binder called Envirobond™ to bind metal contaminants, preventing leaching under the most stringent conditions. Envirobond™ has successfully treated many types of heavy metals at high levels of contamination, including arsenic, chromium, lead, silver, cadmium and zinc. The Envirobond™ binder can be used in two different configurations:

ENVIROBOND™ ON-SURFACE STABILIZATION/COMPACTION

In this technology, the soil and binder mixture is spread on the ground and compacted with heavy equipment. Four steps are involved:

- Excavation of the contaminated soil to the treatment area.
- Addition of Envirobond™ and other additives.
- Tilling and mixing.
- Compaction.

ENVIROBOND™ LOOSE PAK STABILIZATION

In this technology, the soil and binder mixture is placed directly into shipping containers. Loose Pak Stabilization is recommended for sites where disposal costs are not a concern.

The Envirobric™ process uses the non-hazardous chemical binder Envirobond™, with another step added to mechanically compact the waste/Envirobond™ mix to produce a solid, compressed form resembling a construction brick. The final waste form has physical strength similar to a cement brick that permits it to be buried or transported and placed in a disposal facility.

RMRS is just one component of the large team working to make the Rocky Flats site and surrounding area safer for Jefferson County residents. With its combined expertise and a safety record that speaks for itself, Rocky Mountain Remediation Services, L.L.C. is making a difference to all who live in and enjoy the Front Range region.

The Envirobond™/Envirobric™ process provides effective treatment and volume reduction of contaminated soils.

CITY OF WESTMINSTER

Location, financial stability, recreation opportunities, education and a sense of community are just a few of the reasons more than 94,000 people live in Westminster.

Conveniently located between Denver and Boulder on U.S. 36 and Interstate 25, residents and businesses enjoy the multitude of amenities offered in this well-established and progressive metropolitan area.

Westminster is considered one of the most vibrant and flourishing cities in Colorado because of its financial stability and its willingness to reinvest in the community. With an ample inventory of available land along major transportation corridors, ideal opportunities for business development abound.

Corporations seeking to relocate find Westminster's warm welcome and strong values appealing. Sales and use taxes are moderate, and finding qualified personnel eager to work is quite easy. No wonder Westminster has been chosen as home by nearly 250 businesses each year including retailers, national and international firms, high-tech manufacturers and high-quality service providers.

Residents and businesses benefit from the many recreational opportunities offered by the City. Included in its line-up are: the award-winning City Park Recreation Center; 1,200 acres of open space; more than forty miles of multipurpose trails enjoyed by walkers, runners, cyclists, skaters and horseback riders; thirty-five parks with playground facilities and sports courts; four golf courses—three public and one private; Standley Lake Recreation Area; Westminster Mall; the nationally recognized Butterfly Pavilion and Insect Center; the Westminster Promenade—a collection of shops restaurants, office space, an AMC 24-screen theater, a Westin Hotel and conference center, and a three-sheet ice centre. Additionally, newly constructed civic facilities have received environmental and architectural awards which reflect the City's sense of vision.

Westminster's educational opportunities add to the City's near perfect appeal for both families and businesses. Quality elementary, middle and high schools serve thousands of students annually. Front Range Community College, home to the Small Business Development Center which offers service and custom training in a wide range of issues involving international trade and marketing, has received national recognition for development of innovative training programs with local corporations. Three of the University of Colorado's four campuses are within twenty minutes of the City. And Westminster's 76,000 square foot College Hill Library offers

Above: Margaret's Pond at Legacy Ridge—one of the many areas preserved as open space in the City of Westminster.
PHOTO COURTESY OF DAN SIDOR.

Below: City of Westminster's 130-foot bell tower has become a community landmark.

educational references and recreational reading material in print and electronic formats, as well as a special children's reading program, and business resources.

The City boasts a wide variety of housing options from entry level to executive homes. At the top of the list is the award-winning Legacy Ridge community which was recognized by *Professional Builder* Magazine with its "Best in American Living Award." The master-planned, golf-course community, located at 112th Avenue and Lowell Boulevard, was a private-public venture spearheaded by Westminster.

No matter the neighborhood, Westminster creates an authentic hometown environment where neighbors can meet and families can enjoy themselves. Building a high-quality, livable community is the guiding principle for all development in this northwest metropolitan city. The City of Westminster is committed to creating and maintaining a vital economy by retaining and expanding business, promoting the City's amenities and preparing for the future. This combination, along with a well-educated workforce, and high quality of living, creates an ideal business and family environment.

Above: Ball Corporation makes its home in Westminster as do other corporate citizens, such as Lucent Technologies, Western Gas Resources and ConferTech International.

Below, left and right: Use of Standley Lake and City Park Recreation Center keep Westminster residents and surrounding neighbors relaxed and rejuvenated throughout the year.

CITY OF
ARVADA

Above: The Arvada Center for the Arts and Humanities offers a wide array of exhibits, performances and education in the arts.

Below: West Woods Golf Course is ranked as one of the top ten public golf courses in Colorado.

PHOTOS COURTESY OF MICHAEL MAURO

Nestled between the foothills of the Rocky Mountains to the west and metropolitan Denver to the east, Arvada is a thriving suburb of 97,000 citizens who enjoy a safe, beautiful, dynamic, and culturally-rich environment.

Arvada is a mix of old and new. Walking in Olde Town, listed on the National Register of Historic Places, gives the sense of living in a time capsule. The restored buildings that once housed the blacksmith, feed mill, grocery, general store, bank, funeral parlor, and pool hall can still be appreciated.

Having begun as a farming community just a few miles from the first Colorado gold discovery in Ralston Creek, Arvada retains its historical flavor while balancing residential growth with commercial, industrial, and professional office developments to provide jobs and services for residents. Within walking distance of Olde Town is the Arvada Urban Renewal Area with movie theaters, restaurants, and shopping.

Arvada's residential community is crisscrossed by a unique system of creeks and canals, where it is possible to amble along more than 125 miles of hiking, biking and horseback riding trails, and enjoy 131 parks consisting of 895 acres of park area, lakes, and open space. At an elevation of 5,337 feet above sea level, Arvada residents enjoy spectacular views of the mountains. Three outstanding golf courses are conveniently located in Arvada and offer beautiful scenery and challenges for the novice to the professional.

Arvada's crime rate ranks as one of the lowest in Colorado. The Arvada Police Department was the first in Colorado and the thirteenth in the nation accredited under the rigorous standards of the National Commission on Accreditation of Law Enforcement Agencies and strongly supports the philosophies of community policing.

Arvada supports one of the metro area's finest arts centers, The Arvada Center for the Arts and Humanities, which produces a variety of performances annually. The Center features an outdoor amphitheater, home of Colorado's finest outdoor entertainment, as well as two floors of gallery space with rotating exhibitions, an historical museum, and numerous educational events.

Major employers in Arvada are COBE Cardiovascular, Mark VII Equipment, Inc., Sundstrand Fluid Handling, Denver Instrument Company, and Tarco, Inc.

CITY OF LAKEWOOD

With a heritage stretching back to Colorado's earliest gold rush days in the 1860s, the City of Lakewood incorporated June 24, 1969, as a collection of suburban neighborhoods, small commercial centers and rural open space. Since then, Lakewood has grown to become the largest city in Jefferson County and the fourth largest in Colorado, with a population of 140,800 projected for the year 2000. Yet the city still retains much of its small-town flavor and open space.

Lakewood maintains one of the highest ratios of parks and recreation facilities per capita in the country, with more than 6,500 acres of park land and over 80 miles of recreational trails. The city's park system includes everything from small neighborhood parks; to boating, camping, fishing and wildlife in wide-open Bear Creek Lake Park; to the 6,800-foot summit of Green Mountain. Since it opened in 1993, Fox Hollow at Lakewood Golf Course has consistently ranked in surveys as Colorado's favorite public golf course. And as an important gateway to the Rocky Mountains, Lakewood offers unlimited opportunities for outdoor recreation.

The city enjoys a national reputation for its quality of life. Lakewood ranked 18th among America's 200 largest cities in a survey of the best cities for women in the November 1997 issue of *Ladies Home Journal*. Nationally admired for its leadership and innovation, the Lakewood Police Department was named one of the country's best suburban police departments in the November 1996 issue of *Good*

Housekeeping. Building strong, safe Lakewood neighborhoods, through close cooperation and planning with residents, is a major focus of city government.

Lakewood is home to the Denver Federal Center, the largest concentration of federal government offices outside of Washington, D.C., employing more than 5,200 people. Striving to be business-friendly, Lakewood's other major employers include medical equipment manufacturers, health care, energy, insurance and financial services, industrial engineering and more. The Lakewood Industrial Park attracts new businesses and jobs, while COBE Laboratories, one of the Park's major, longtime companies, continues to expand with a new 60,000 square foot medical sterilization facility. With a well-educated workforce, Lakewood provides an ideal environment for high-tech companies such as the Colorado Bio/Medical Venture Center, a business development enterprise for young bio/medical companies, housed at Lakewood's AMC Cancer Research Center campus.

A $3 million capital campaign by Lakewood's Heritage Center typifies Lakewood as the twentieth century draws to a close. The campaign will fund major expansions to preserve Lakewood's history, as well as provide major community facilities for the future, including a 500-seat outdoor amphitheater. Likewise, proud of its past, Lakewood stands poised with the rest of Jefferson County on the threshold of a new century.

COALITION OF JEFFERSON COUNTY CHAMBERS OF COMMERCE

The five Chambers that make up the Coalition of Jefferson County Chambers of Commerce have been collaborating and coordinating on business issues of common interest to Jefferson County businesses since the late 1980's. This active group of Chambers, consisting of Conifer, Evergreen Area, Greater Golden, Northwest Metro and West, formally incorporated in 1995 as a way to formalize its combined efforts and serve as a stronger force in representing its members. Today, the Coalition represents over 3000 employers in Jefferson County.

The Coalition of Jefferson County Chambers was established for the purpose of serving as a unified voice for all businesses within Jefferson County. Its focus is to promote business and community growth through civic, social and cultural programs while enhancing the value of each participating community. With special emphasis on the economic, commercial, industrial and education interests of Jefferson County, the group formulates position statements and creates action plans to address the common concerns of the surrounding region.

Individual members of the five participating Chambers have been enhanced by the coordinated efforts of the Coalition. For example, rather than each Chamber holding a committee meeting on an area of concern, the group coordinates on regional matters such as transportation, education and state legislative lobbying activities on behalf of all Chamber members. While the Coalition remains autonomous from local Chambers in developing issues, it relies on support from each organization for funding and leadership.

The leadership or chairmanship of the Coalition rotates yearly from Chamber to Chamber with individual Chambers maintaining an equal vote in determining policies and program direction. Board members from each of the five Chambers are selected to serve as Coalition representatives under the leadership of the Executive Committee Chair from the guiding Chamber. It is the guiding Chamber that then supplies administrative support during its year of leadership.

All individuals involved in the Coalition of Jefferson County Chambers are dedicated to enhancing the quality of life in the Jefferson County region. Together, they are helping to take care of business for the communities they serve.

NORTHWEST METRO CHAMBER

GREATER GOLDEN CHAMBER

THE WEST CHAMBER

EVERGREEN AREA CHAMBER

CONIFER CHAMBER

CHURCH RANCH

In 1861, George Henry Church came to this area with ox drawn wagons from Independence, Iowa. In the spring of 1864, the Church family became the first homesteaders in Jefferson County. They built a house on Walnut Creek which became known as Church's Crossing and subsequently the first stop on the overland Stagecoach Route from Denver to Boulder—a two-day excursion. As the years progressed, the Church's were also the first to bring irrigation and Hereford cattle into Colorado.

Charles C. McKay, a fourth generation Church, has been continuing his family's entrepreneurial ambitions for the past twenty years by maintaining the Hereford cattle operation, developing mineral ownerships, and developing three business parks within the north Denver metropolitan area which offer land sales, build to suit, and leasing opportunities.

Church Ranch Corporate Center, a 143-acre, mixed use development located in Westminster, is designed to harmonize with the environment; the park contains pedestrian/nature trails and ponds. In July of 1998, McKay and his partner, Gregg A. Bradbury, completed the 126,550 square foot Church Ranch Business Center and are pleased to say it is 100% leased. Tenants include Advantage Computing, All American Semi-Conductors, Children's Hospital, Itelco USA, Level 3 Communications, Marshall Industries, and MC Technology. Other projects Church Ranch has underway include: a 207,500 square foot Church Ranch Office Center; two 65,000 square foot office buildings; and two 126,000 square foot buildings to house offices, a hotel and a restaurant; all to be completed with its new partner, the Etkin-Johnson Group.

Church Ranch Industrial Center and Church Ranch Tech Center are two additional new developments. The 138-acre Industrial Center is a masterplanned industrial development along Highway 93, allowing easy access to the neighboring cities of Boulder and Golden. This site features one mile of rail frontage, ample utilities and raw water. The site is at the base of the eastern slope of the Rocky Mountains with incredible mountain views.

The 158-acre Church Ranch Tech Center is a mixed use development site in Arvada and offers development, land sales, build to suit, office space, R&D, warehouse and light industrial leasing. This project's best asset is its location with magnificent views of Standley Lake, Denver, the eastern slope, exceptional high plains and mountain character.

Being in the right place at the right time with the right development products is what Church Ranch and its forefathers has been about for well over 130 years. A long-time resident of Jefferson County, Church Ranch plans to continue its contributions to this area for years to come.

Above: 1998 Construction of the Church Ranch Office Center, Westminster (Jefferson County).

Below: Perry Sidway McKay, Katherine Church and Charles Church McKay.

STOCKTON PET HOSPITAL

The health of a pet and its owner is predicated by knowledge, concern, commitment and support. The staff at Stockton Pet Hospital in Lakewood is dedicated to providing all this and more to ensure the quality of your companion's life.

Stockton Pet Hospital was started in 1965 by Dr. Nell Stockton, one of the first women to attend Colorado State University's School of Veterinary Medicine. Dr. Stockton began her business from her small home on South Wadsworth, which still serves as the hospital's grooming facility.

In 1985, Dr. William Wilcox, DVM, and his wife, Verla, purchased the veterinary practice. Today, it has grown over four-fold for several significant reasons.

SENSITIVITY

As with many well-established and flourishing businesses, Dr. Stockton's practice was based on loyalty and longevity. That meant the majority of her clients had older pets. Recognizing the special place pets hold in the hearts of many people, the Wilcox's began offering regularly scheduled pet loss seminars, one of the first clinics in the area to do so. This sensitivity supports pet owners in understanding and coping with their loss.

Above: Verla and Dr. William Wilcox offer the most appropriate treatment for each animal they see.

Below: Stockton Pet Hospital is located at 1234 South Wadsworth Boulevard in Lakewood.

CUSTOMER SERVICE

Again, as one of the first clinics in the area, Stockton Pet Hospital extended its office hours to accommodate the varied schedules of pet owners. The hospital is open Monday through Friday, 7:30 a.m. to 7:00 p.m., and Saturdays, 8:00 a.m. to 4:00 p.m., with a doctor available during most of that time. The clinic's policy is to see a sick pet the same day an owner calls. An RN with emergency room experience serves as a receptionist to help determine the urgency in getting a pet to the hospital.

APPROACH

Dr. Wilcox and his staff continuously work to integrate both conventional and holistic aspects of healthcare for animals. While 95% of the hospital's focus is on conventional medicine, another 5% involves other healthcare options. As society becomes more aware of and open to the benefits of alternatives in healthcare, pet owners are following suit. Dr. Wilcox works closely with a qualified chiropractor, acupuncturist, osteopath and massage therapist to offer the most appropriate and beneficial treatment for individual animals.

As with humans, many problems can be eliminated and the recovery of certain conditions enhanced through proper nutrition and the use of supplements. Whether treating a lizard that needs calcium supplements to strengthen its bones or a dog that requires chiropractic adjustments to prevent seizures, the staff at Stockton Pet Hospital shares knowledge, concern, commitment and support to pets and their owners throughout Jefferson County.

The guidelines under which Hank Vecchiarelli started Hank's Auto Body in 1950 were simple: Do your business. Do your job. Focus on customers and quality. They are the same guidelines Hank's son, Tony, and grandson, Vince, follow in their management of the business today, with results that speak for themselves.

Located at 4890 Robb Street in Wheat Ridge, Hank's Auto Body West is one of the largest collision-only repair facilities in Colorado and ranks in the top ten in the United States. Nearly 350 vehicles are serviced each month out of the seventy-two bay, 42,000-square foot facility.

But for Tony and Vince, the business is not about having the largest complex or seeing how many cars they can push through the system. It is about providing the kind of service that offers a customer reassurance after his car has been damaged. Whether repairing a small scratch or completing a major collision repair, the staff at Hank's Auto Body West is dedicated to making sure the work is done right the first time and the experience is as smooth and comfortable as possible.

"People aren't happy when they first call us or walk through the front door," says Tony, who opened the Robb Street location in 1983. "That's why we have to do what's right." And that means every employee must work together to assure customers their cars will be fixed, their needs will be met, all to their satisfaction. Guaranteed.

As a value-added service, Hank's Auto Body West offers the convenience of car rental service through its facility; it was one of the first body shops in the area to do so.

To Tony and Vince, providing a supportive environment for employees is just as important as strong customer satisfaction. The company offers its employees ongoing training, access to the latest technology and equipment, opportunity for job advancement, clean working conditions and an in-house gym facility. Workers know they will be listened to when they approach management with their concerns and suggestions for how things are done.

The Vecchiarelli's reputation for fairness goes beyond their many satisfied customers and workers. Hank's Auto Body West was named Small Business of the Year in 1995 by the West Chamber of Commerce. It has received the Industry Recognition Award for contributing to economic growth in Jefferson County. It has also received the Clean Air Colorado and Corporate Alliance for Better Air Award.

Hank's Auto Body West is a Jefferson County company that is here to stay. A name you can count on, with service you can trust.

HANK'S AUTO BODY WEST

Hank's Auto Body West, located along North Frontage Road between Kipling Street and Ward Road.

JEFFERSON COUNTY AIRPORT

Above: Jeffco Airport is Colorado's fourth busiest airport, averaging 157,000 departures and arrivals per year.

Below: With its prime location in north Jefferson County, Jeffco Airport is Denver's premier corporate reliever airport, providing convenient access to Boulder and Denver.

PHOTOS COURTESY OF JIM YOST

Jefferson County (Jeffco) Airport is Denver's premier corporate reliever airport. Ideally situated between Denver and Boulder on U.S. 36, Jeffco is the closest airport to both cities, placing travelers just minutes from the area's major business parks, universities and recreational facilities.

Jeffco Airport was established in 1960 and has been self-supporting for over thirty years. The airport does not receive local tax dollars for funding; rather, revenues are generated by user fees, land leases and fuel tax. In 1965, the Jefferson County Airport Authority was created to set airport policies and regulations. This five member team of volunteers is elected by the Jefferson County Commissioners to serve four-year terms and preside as the decision-makers for growth, expansion and to ensure adherence to high safety standards for pilots, travelers and workers.

As Colorado's fourth busiest airport, Jeffco Airport averages 157,000 departures and arrivals per year, with the majority of traffic being corporate or business related. This ranks the airport in the top one percent of 17,000 airports nationwide.

Jeffco's 25,000 square foot Terminal Building is equipped with a wide range of amenities for both business and leisure travelers. A cafe-style restaurant serves sandwiches and daily specials and has catering available for on-board flights and special occasions. The passenger waiting area is a delightful place to relax with its expansive view of the Rocky Mountains. The Terminal Building also has conference rooms available for rent, making this a great place for business and social groups to meet. Groups ranging in size from twelve to 100 will find the accommodations comfortable and offer the privacy desired.

Jeffco Airport is open twenty-four hours a day with an FAA Control Tower in operation from 6 a.m. to 10 p.m. seven days a week for safer departures and landings. An on-site U.S. Customs facility operates regular hours Monday through Friday and on a call-out basis after hours and on weekends. Two Fixed Base Operators provide airport customers with av gas, jet fuel, aircraft and avionics maintenance, turbine engine overhaul, hangar space, flight instruction, rental and charter service.

The airport's highly efficient operations are due, in part, to its prime location in north Jefferson County. The airspace around Jeffco does not interfere with flight patterns at Denver International Airport, allowing controllers to give priority to the airport's traffic.

With the corporate headquarters of Ball Corporation and its convenient access for surrounding high tech companies such as Storage Tek, Level 3 Communications, Pentax Technologies, Corporate Express and Sun Microsystems, it's little wonder Jefferson County Airport has become Denver's Corporate Choice.

Camden Property Trust, headquartered in Houston, Texas, is a fully integrated real estate investment trust (REIT) engaged in the ownership, development, acquisition, marketing, management and disposition of multi-family apartment communities.

Camden merged with Oasis Residential, Inc. in April 1998 and operates in Denver as Camden Development, Inc. The company's Denver portfolio consists of six former Oasis properties along with the newest Camden development, The Greens at Interlocken.

The Greens at Interlocken is a beautiful, resort-style master planned community located on Eldorado Boulevard in Broomfield. The property sits adjacent to the Interlocken golf course and offers majestic views of the Flat Iron Mountains. The community features a spectacular pool, spa, fitness center, business center and resident billiards room. The interior of the apartment homes offer nine-foot ceilings, oversized tubs, walk-in closets and gas fireplaces along with an attached garage to each unit.

Other Camden communities in Denver include elegant lakeside living at The Park at Lakeway, located in Littleton on Wadsworth and Belleview, and an exciting family-style planned community featuring three-bedroom apartment homes with a variety of innovative services and children's facilities at The Park at Deerwood in Highlands Ranch.

In Westminster, Camden operates two communities: The Park at Wexford located on 123rd and Huron, and Park Place located on 116th and Huron. Both offer spacious one- and two-bedroom floor plans, gracious amenities and easy access to Boulder, Denver and Denver International Airport.

Camden's apartment communities offer six to twelve month leases on unfurnished homes. It also provides corporate housing packages for those needing fully furnished homes for a shorter period of time.

In any of Camden's conveniently located and relaxing communities, residents find exceptional service from the on-site staff in addition to an outstanding apartment they can call home.

Camden Property Trust—Living Up to Your Standards.

Top, left: The Park at Deerwood in Highlands Ranch on University south of C-470.

Top, right: Residential clubhouse at The Park at Lakeway.

Below: The Park at Lakeway in Grant Ranch on Wadsworth and Belleview.

FOOTHILLS PARK & RECREATION DISTRICT

Above: The Meadows Golf Club is a very popular public golf facility that offers a driving range, pro shop, restaurant and both eighteen- and nine-hole regulation courses.

Bottom, right: Clement Park, one of three regional parks in the Foothills district, provides sports fields, playgrounds, picnic shelters, tennis courts, trails, a lake and open space with a great view of the foothills.

Bottom, left: Lilley Gulch Recreation Center provides gym space, an indoor pool, racquetball courts, daycare/preschool and a wide variety of recreation programs for all ages.

South Jeffco Metropolitan Recreation and Park District was created on December 31, 1959. Renamed Foothills in 1970, the District manages sixty-three neighborhood parks, three regional parks, twenty-three miles of trails, fourteen reservoirs/conservation areas, and serves a population of nearly 160,000 residents within forty-four square miles. The red rocks of the hogback provide a spectacular backdrop for its geographical boundaries which are Sixth Avenue on the north, Sheridan Boulevard on the east, Chatfield on the south and the hogback on the west.

The District is governed by a five member Board of Directors, elected at large to four-year terms. It operates on a $12 million budget, 72% of which is derived from fees and charges, and the remaining 28% from property tax. Eighty-five full-time and 350 hourly/seasonal employees make up the District's staff.

Many of the District's outstanding facilities have been built with the assistance of local sports associations, private citizen donations, and private sector land donations. Denver Water, Land and Water Conservation, Jefferson County Open Space, The Colorado Lottery, and The Foothills Foundation are just a few of its loyal supporters. The Foundation is dedicated specifically to promoting and providing increased leisure opportunities to the Foothills District through its fundraising efforts and has raised over $1 million since its inception in 1988.

Foothills' recreation facilities include fifty-four holes of golf, ten lighted ball fields, and seven swimming pools. Over 400 programs are offered at various locations for all ages. Classes range from aquatics, art, senior trips and wellness programs to numerous sports including gymnastics and golf.

Foothills District was the recipient of the prestigious National Recreation and Park Association (NRPA) Gold Medal Award for Excellence in Recreation and Park Management in 1986 and 1991.

It has received the NRPA Excellence in Aquatics Award in both 1993 and 1998. It has also been recognized nationally and by the Colorado Park and Recreation Association for its leadership and innovation in programs such as the comprehensive Wellness Program, Moving for Life and Active Options Senior Program, the Well Kids Heart Healthy Program, and Silence the Violence and Neutral Zone Teen Programs.

On January 1, 2001, Foothills District will move its operations south of Hampden Avenue. A November 4, 1997 citizen vote determined that the area north of Hampden (which has historically been serviced by both Foothills and the City of Lakewood), will now be maintained and operated by the City of Lakewood alone. Foothills Park and Recreation District will continue to provide major recreation facilities and a wide range of recreation programming to over 95,000 residents in South Jefferson County.

Considered the "tow truck czar" in the Denver metro area, George Connolly has earned his title after twenty-five years in the towing industry. Mr. Connolly has personally assisted in a wide range of towing incidents across the greater Denver area, many of which have involved serious and even hazardous conditions.

Mr. Connolly started Connolly's Towing in July of 1973 with one Dodge wrecker. In 1979, after operating out of a rented storage facility and sharing a radio with another towing company for a short time, he purchased industrial acreage with a house on the premises located at 5702 West 60th Avenue. This remains the company's headquarters today. For ten years George and his wife, Cynthia, raised three children in this home while running their towing business from a small office in the back of the house.

In 1992, Mr. Connolly purchased Griff's Towing Service which had four trucks and was located at 42nd and McIntyre. Connolly ran both businesses until incorporating several years later. Today, Connolly's Towing employs twenty-nine people and services over 200 accounts. It has a fleet of sixteen towing trucks and three service trucks to assist in jobs involving the smallest car to the largest semi. The company's newest vehicle, Bruno, weighs forty-five tons and can lift 90,000 pounds.

Highly dedicated to giving back to the community, Connolly's donates vehicles to all surrounding police and fire departments for use in training. In addition, the yard is used by area police agencies for training canine units. The company donates wrecked vehicles to areas schools for drinking and driving awareness programs and trucks for use in the Arvada Harvest Festival. It also sponsors an Arvada softball team, contributes to the Drug Awareness Resistance Education (D.A.R.E.). program, and recently restored an abandoned trailer that was donated to the Boy Scouts of America.

Mr. Connolly serves as president of the Towing and Recovery Professionals of Colorado. He has been a member since 1978. With the help of other reputable Colorado towers, the association worked with the Public Utilities Commission to revise its rules and regulations, resulting in policies that benefit towers at both the state and local levels.

Many people in Jefferson County know Connolly's Towing for the tremendous number of hours provided to the community. But the hallmark for which Mr. Connolly takes the greatest pride is his restored 1929 Ford with a 485 Holmes wrecker. This vehicle has won many local and national awards and will soon go on display for two years in the International Towing and Recovery Hall of Fame and Museum in Chattanooga, Tennessee.

Above: Bruno, Connolly's newest addition to the fleet.

Below: William James Connolly, George and Cynthia's grandson, standing proudly on the running board of the restored 1929 Ford with 485 Holmes wrecker.

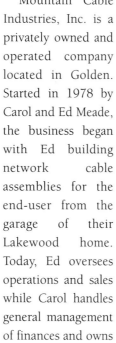

MOUNTAIN CABLE INDUSTRIES, INC.

Mountain Cable Industries, Inc. is a privately owned and operated company located in Golden. Started in 1978 by Carol and Ed Meade, the business began with Ed building network cable assemblies for the end-user from the garage of their Lakewood home. Today, Ed oversees operations and sales while Carol handles general management of finances and owns 51% of the corporation, making Mountain Cable a "Minority Woman Business Enterprise." Working side by side from their foundation of many years, the Meades have guided their company through numerous changes.

Soon after Mountain Cable's inception, business increased and Ed began taking in larger orders which proved to be too much work for just two people. Ed looked to Green Mountain High School and found help from several students who were happy to join the payroll for extra spending money.

Eventually, it was time to expand out of the garage. Upon approval from the company's advisory board of directors, the decision was made in 1981 to purchase a 6,700 square foot facility at the current West 5th Avenue location.

Since that time, the business has grown ravenously. Five new additions to the original building have brought the facili-ty to 21,000 square feet with nearly seventy employees operating up to three shifts at various times throughout the year.

Mountain Cable builds a wide array of custom and standard cable assemblies, both copper and fiber, for the data, telephony, O.E.M., CATV and DBS satellite markets. In addition, it builds coaxial jumpers and custom satellite installation kits. The production facility can process over one million feet of cable in roughly forty-eight hours.

Contributing to the education of the local youth as well as sponsoring several local charities are high priorities for Mountain Cable. Mr. Meade willingly donates his time presenting seminars about entrepreneurship to area schools and eagerly employs highly motivated and bright young people who want to learn about life in the business arena.

In today's world, technical advances stops for no one. Therefore, as times and technologies change, so does Mountain Cable Industries. It is a leader in design, engineering, manufacturing, and testing. With inventors rapidly creating new technologies, Mountain Cable has the capabilities to assist in almost any cabling application from idea to prototype to production. Mountain Cable Industries' commitment to excellence and quality lives up to its motto "We Link Technologies".

Above: Network production area preparing and building cable assemblies.

Below: CATV/DBS connectorization of cable assemblies.

JEHN & ASSOCIATES, INC.

Aesthetically pleasing and environmentally responsive. These are the results clients expect when Jehn & Associates, Inc. is involved in a land development/engineering project. With a solid reputation for technical expertise, the company prides itself in its ability to work through environmentally sensitive challenges, turning engineered infrastructures into showcase settings. West Woods Golf Course in Arvada, awarded for its environmental excellence, and the Star Guide Lake area in Wheat Ridge are prime examples of the outstanding work by Jehn & Associates.

Founded in 1982 by Joseph A. Jehn, P.E., the company has served over 800 clients throughout the United States and Canada, and as far away as American Samoa. Committed to operating as a full-service civil engineering, surveying and construction management firm, clients seek out Jehn & Associates for its diligence and professionalism.

The company offers the advantage of in-house coordination of all disciplines, including management of the entitlement process, a key element that places Jehn & Associates in high standing with its clients. Commercial, institutional, governmental, municipal, private, industrial and religious organizations alike know they can count on Jehn & Associates to obtain the necessary approvals for their specialized projects, large or small. Mr. Jehn's knowledge, problem solving ability and tenacity insure that even the most com-

plex projects become a reality with all parties being satisfied in the end. The company has a nearly 100% track record to date.

Jehn & Associates uses the latest GPS surveying technology along with other state-of-the-art equipment and software. The use of these tools expands capabilities and results in dramatic productivity gains as staff members complete projects with a high level of efficiency and accuracy.

Strongly committed to Jefferson County, Joseph A. Jehn brings a wealth of knowledge and experience to issues that focus on community growth and prosperity. He has been involved, at various levels, in each of the following: Jefferson County Open Space Advisory Committee, Jefferson County Task Force for Youth Sports Fields, Forward Arvada Building Corporation, Arvada Youth Foundation, Olde Town Arvada Business Improvement District and Westminster's Board of Building Code Appeals.

Above, left: Water feature with water quality and detention, West Woods Golf Course.

Above, right: Church Ditch golf cart crossing, West Woods Golf Course.

Below: Star Guide Corporation World Headquarters.

EASTER-OWENS

Easter-Owens began as a metal-fabrication business in Denver in 1955. Started by Bill Easter and Al Owens, their vision was to provide a new level of service and quality to local electricians. In the nearly half century since then, Easter-Owens has expanded from a small, local company serving a single market to a nationally known design, engineering and manufacturing firm which produces high-quality products for a long list of loyal customers.

Easter-Owens' manufacturing capabilities range from simple junction boxes to complex monitoring and control systems. Its systems are used around the world in a wide range of industries including mining, oil and gas, food and beverage, material handling, utilities, defense, aerospace, and most notably, prison security. The company's diversification into the detention market has become a special niche for Easter-Owens, gaining them national recognition in the industry.

The Arvada company employs seventy highly skilled and experienced designers and engineers. A project begins with client-provided specifications or a general description of the desired end-product. Drawings are created, with engineers and designers often recommending cost saving modifications. The process then continues in a unique manner, without the use of assembly lines. Each project is assigned to one of several fabricators who takes sole responsibility for the product from layout through final assembly, performing a number of critical operations at each step along the way.

All workers at Easter-Owens are skilled in a range of trades, disciplines and activities. They take great pride in their craftsmanship and are committed to meeting the often stringent deadlines of their clients while maintaining product quality and integrity.

A sister organization, Integrated Systems Incorporated, with offices in Texas and Michigan, was established in 1994 to provide customers with continuity over the life of the projects first undertaken by Easter-Owens. Operating as a turn-key systems integrator, Integrated Systems Incorporated offers on-going support to clients with design, installation and service needs within the integrated security and life safety systems arena. Services include card access, photo imaging, CCTV, intercom and sound communications, intrusion monitoring and control, and fire safety. Always conscious of a customer's budget, the company installs systems to meet the individual cost and service criterion of those they serve.

Working together, Easter-Owens and Integrated Systems Incorporated remain committed to providing quality manufacturing services, unique solutions and long-term value that stand heads above the crowd. Customers simply will not find higher quality at any price, anywhere.

Above: Industrial control system for City of Los Angeles, California.

Below: Easter-Owens' headquarters in Arvada, Colorado.

Walking through the doors of Pickering's Automotive & Transmission's new location at 90 South Wadsworth Boulevard is like a trip back to the fifties. Complete with soda fountain style counter, checkered floor and forty-fives reminiscent of the era tacked to the walls, the inside is hoppin', friendly and clean.

While Pickering's location and look are new, loyal customers will find the changes stop there. The store's service is the same as customers have come to trust and appreciate since Randy and Lynette Pickering began their business over fifteen years ago.

Well-established in the community, Pickering's is a complete automotive and transmission service center and operates as a registered NAPA Auto Care Center and Air Care Colorado emissions repair location. It is a member of the Automotive Service Association (ASA) and has received ASA's Gold Medallion rating for excellence.

As an AAA Approved Auto Repair facility, Pickering's has maintained a high customer satisfaction rating as surveyed by AAA each month. As added service, Pickering's Automotive & Transmission offers its cus-tomers rides to and from its facility to accommodate their schedules and will arrange for car rental as needed. It offers to perform a complimentary 30-point vehicle inspection upon every vehicle that arrives in the shop. And regardless of whether Pickering's performs the follow-up work, the results of the inspection are recorded and discussed with the customer.

Pickering's technicians, all ASE certified, work in an immaculate fifteen-bay facility. Already highly qualified, the majority hold the classification of L1 and Master Certified Technician.

Although Randy grew up in a form of the automotive industry, he is not a technician by trade. His experience comes from sales and customer service which shows in his dedication to providing the kind of service that keeps his business growing and retaining satisfied customers. This dedication is also apparent through interaction with the service advisors and technicians who are committed to "getting the job done right, on time, the first time."

With state-of-the-art equipment at hand and by staying current on the latest changes in the rapidly moving automotive industry, Pickering's Automotive & Transmission, Inc. provides superior service, honest value and a fun place to take your car.

PICKERING'S AUTOMOTIVE & TRANSMISSION, INC.

Above: Depicting the nostalgia of the fifties, Pickering's offers quality service and honest value.

Below: Celebrating over fifteen years in business at its new location.

PHOTOS COURTESY OF SHELLEY WALLEN.

NORTH JEFFCO PARK & RECREATION DISTRICT

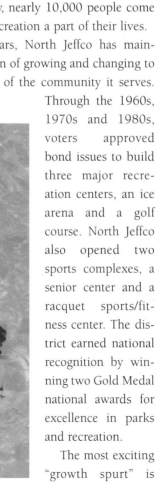

North Jeffco Park and Recreation District came into being in 1956, when a group of citizens banded together to make Arvada a better place for its citizens and children. Soon afterward, North Jeffco was created as a special district and in 1958, opened its first facility: the outdoor pool at North Jeffco Park on Ralston Road just east of Garrison Street.

The pool still draws large, enthusiastic crowds all summer long… and, today, the district also operates nineteen year-round and seasonal facilities in a sixty square-mile area in northeast Jefferson County. It shares in the management of 125 miles of trails and 131 parks and open space areas. Every day, nearly 10,000 people come here to make recreation a part of their lives.

Over the years, North Jeffco has maintained a tradition of growing and changing to meet the needs of the community it serves. Through the 1960s, 1970s and 1980s, voters approved bond issues to build three major recreation centers, an ice arena and a golf course. North Jeffco also opened two sports complexes, a senior center and a racquet sports/fitness center. The district earned national recognition by winning two Gold Medal national awards for excellence in parks and recreation.

The most exciting "growth spurt" is going on right now. It began in the mid-1990s, when the district made nearly $4 million worth of improvements and additions and set the stage for several new facilities. Combining its resources with additional funding from sources such as Jefferson County Open Space and the Colorado Lottery, North Jeffco built a new six-field ballfield complex, a new teen center, and made major improvements at many other facilities.

In May 1998, voters approved a $25 million bond issue for a new 140,000 square foot community center, initial development of Long Lake Ranch athletic complex, and improvements to two other facilities. As the new century unfolds, participants will be drawn to North Jeffco from around the region, particularly to the community center with its twin sheets of ice, indoor aquatic playground and assortment of activities for every age.

It is hard to imagine that it all started with a handful of concerned citizens and a $15,000 bank loan. But in some ways, things are not so different than they were in 1956. The North Jeffco Park and Recreation District is still in the business of helping the community and the people who live here, and it still reflects the active, enthusiastic community it serves.

Above: Indian Tree Golf Course, 7555 Wadsworth Boulevard.

Below: Enjoying the water at Lake Arbor outdoor pool, 7451 West 83rd Way.

It has become a place where one can find furniture, place settings, decorative accessories—almost everything for a Rocky Mountain home, artfully displayed.

The Hardware has been squeezed into the old Hiwan Barn where every nook and cranny is utilized for inventory. Downstairs you will find all of the tools and materials to complete a job, large or small. Upstairs you will find an outlet for the more creative urges—a place where you can define how you want your home to look.

The heritage in Evergreen lives on even through the inevitable changes that time requires. In The Hardware and at Mountain Home, customers will encounter the same friendly service, a sense of community and an inspired approach to mountain living that has been constantly expressed for seventy-five years.

Above: Mountain Home's decorative accessories and artful furnishings will splendidly complement any Rocky Mountain home.

Below: With a seventy-five year history, The Hardware continues to provide an inspired approach to mountain living.

The Hardware and Mountain Home have been central businesses in Evergreen for seventy-five years. Today, both stores are owned and operated by Ted La Montagne and his wife, Kay D'Evelyn La Montagne. The success and growth of these enterprises have been founded on the desire to serve the customer and the community as a whole.

The Hardware began in 1924 as Evergreen Transfer, transporting livestock, delivering luggage and carting the community Christmas tree to its honored post in the center of town. As Evergreen has changed and grown over the years, so has The Hardware, by evolving to meet the needs of the community.

A complementary extension of The Hardware is Mountain Home. This home accessory store is adjacent to The Hardware and is housed in the remodeled bunkhouse of the historic Hiwan Homestead.

CARROLL & LANGE, INC.

Quality service, fairness and attention to communication are the key success factors of Carroll & Lange, Inc., a locally owned general/civil engineering firm. The company was founded in 1984 in Lakewood by John Carroll and Jerald Lange. In 1997, a second office was opened in Winter Park, continuing the offering of quality development services throughout the state of Colorado.

Carroll & Lange, Inc. is one of the largest firms of its kind in the Denver metropolitan area. With a staff of 100 highly qualified professional, technical and survey personnel, design teams are created to meet the specific needs of each client and project within many municipalities and public agencies.

From feasibility and drainage studies to development plans and construction administration, Carroll & Lange, Inc. represents both the private and public sectors with commitment and dedication to providing a quality product in a timely manner and at a competitive price.

Communication is the cornerstone of Carroll & Lange, Inc.'s service, and the company as a whole brings the highest level of design and development to the projects it undertakes.

Carroll & Lange, Inc. is proud to be part of two outstanding Jefferson County planned communities, Grant Ranch and Wyndham Park. Together, these two communities won nineteen Mame Awards presented by the Home Builders Association for excellence in 1996 and 1997.

Other notable Jefferson County developments include such projects as Brookhill Shopping Center, Medved Autoplex, Chatfield Green, and Foothills Park and Recreation facilities.

Top to bottom:

Grant Ranch Village Center.

Grant Ranch Open Space.

Wyndham Park Community Entry.

Medved Autoplex.

K/S CONSTRUCTION SERVICES, INC.

Commitment to Excellence. K/S Construction Services, Inc., a general contracting firm based in Lakewood, has maintained its commitment to quality service since its inception in 1988. No matter the level of challenge, K/S Construction has repeatedly proven its ability to provide excellent general contracting services to its clients.

K/S Construction provides demolition, remodeling and renovation with a primary focus on projects involving office and retail space, medical facilities, schools and restaurants. While tenant finish and renovation have been at the company's core for continuous growth and stability since it opened its doors, K/S Construction has developed a track record for excellence in ground-up construction; guaranteeing on-time turnover of projects.

Maintaining an impressive list of repeat clientele, K/S Construction completes numerous commercial, institutional, light industrial and residential projects each year. Hallmarks to the company's credit include: Elevator remodel and exterior canopy addition for the United States Postal Service in Boulder and Fort Collins; interior finish to Crawford Elementary School in Aurora; completion of an addition to Fairview Elementary School in Westminster; an addition and renovation of Montview Elementary School in Aurora; restaurant tenant finishes for Tera Nova Industries including Alcatraz Brewing, California Café and Sevilla at The Ice House in Denver; addition and interior finish to Manor Care Health Services in Boulder and Denver; and interior custom trim and millwork for Adams Mark Hotel in Denver.

K/S Construction employs a full-time staff of twenty individuals, including highly qualified managerial and administrative personnel as well as a technically skilled labor force comprised of carpenters, general construction laborers and maintenance technicians. Combined, the management staff has over sixty years of experience in the construction industry.

Focused on satisfying its customers, K/S Construction Services, Inc. has structured safety and quality control procedures to assure that all projects are completed on time and within budget. Material and equipment purchases are handled in an efficient manner, and detailed schedules are compiled to allow for proper construction sequencing. The company is bonded within limits appropriate to all building needs and has an established line of credit with its bank.

K/S Construction Services, Inc. is available to serve its customers. Let them demonstrate their abilities either with negotiated or bid work.

Above: California Café, Park Meadows Mall.

Below: Alzheimer Suite at Manor Care Health Services, Denver.

COBE/ GAMBRO HEALTHCARE

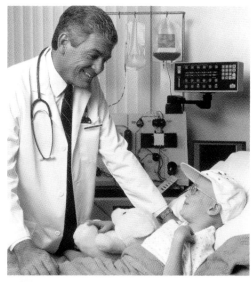

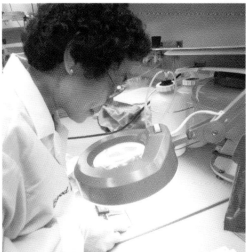

Patients around the world have benefited from COBE/GAMBRO Healthcare technology and research.

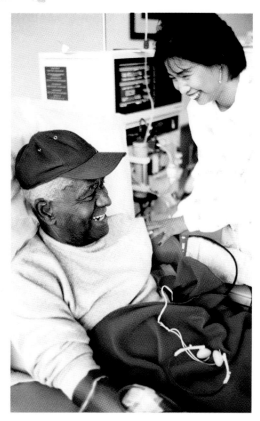

COBE/GAMBRO Healthcare is a charter member of the Jefferson County Coalition of Chambers. The company is recognized as an environmentally responsible corporate citizen and is a recipient of The Colorado Governor's Pollution Prevention Partnership Award.

The U.S. Gambro companies were founded as COBE Laboratories in California in 1964. COBE moved to Jefferson County in 1968. In 1990, COBE was acquired by the Swedish firm, Gambro AB. Today, the U.S. Gambro group is made up of three internationally recognized medical technology companies and an international sales and marketing business that service medical facilities and patients in over 90 countries.

Together, these companies deliver life-saving equipment and medical services to patients throughout the world. The U.S. Gambro group employs 2,000 people in Jefferson County and over 15,000 globally.

COBE BCT, INC.

COBE BCT provides innovative products for blood banking and cancer therapy. BCT and its customers are working together to establish BCT's automated blood component collection technique as a new standard for blood donations. The technique allows more blood to be collected from fewer donors, making transfusion safer and more efficient.

COBE CARDIOVASCULAR, INC.

COBE Cardiovascular manufactures heart/ lung machines, oxygenators, custom tubing packs, and blood processing equipment for surgical applications. In an increasingly cost-conscious market, COBE Cardiovascular works to advance medical technology while finding ways to reduce costs for the patient.

GAMBRO HEALTHCARE

GAMBRO Healthcare is a leading manufacturer of dialysis equipment and the second largest dialysis provider in the world. The company offers disease management services to the healthcare profession. Because of its patient focus and partnerships with leading university medical research centers, GAMBRO Healthcare continues to improve the quality of life for dialysis patients and their families.

COBE INTERNATIONAL

COBE International provides overseas marketing, sales and manufacturing services to the U.S. Gambro group companies, as well as overseas clinical services for dialysis patients.

MILE-HI MACHINE, INC.

With a thirty-year history in the Denver metropolitan area, Mile-Hi Machine, Inc. resonates quality, team work and strong family commitment.

Mike G. Szabo, founder of Mile-Hi Machine, Inc., came to the United States from Europe with his family in 1957. Twelve years later, after working for United Airlines and FTS Corporation, later known as Chaparral Industries, Mike started Mile-Hi Machine & Mold. Upon its inception, the company supplied molded component parts to Gates Rubber in addition to supplying precision parts to companies in the aerospace industry.

In 1979, Mile-Hi Machine & Mold incorporated and the name was changed to Mile-Hi Machine, Inc. No longer involved in mold work, Mile-Hi Machine continues to provide precision machined parts to a wide representation of industries in the medical, aerospace and computer arenas. Loyal government and commercial customers include: Hill Air Force Base, O.E.A., Lockheed Martin, Stanley Aviation, Medex, Metrum, Honeywell, Micro Switch, Loral and Ball Container. Mile-Hi Machine's recent focus on supplying parts for Hewlett Packard's exclusive computer cooling systems has led to serving other high-end computer markets as well.

Originally located on Speer Boulevard, Mile-Hi Machine moved to Arvada in 1980 with the help of the Urban Renewal Authority. The transition was easy since the Szabos and their four children, all of whom are involved in the business today, live in the area. Now located at 6395 West 56th Avenue, Mile-Hi Machine employs up to thirty-five people. The strong economy and high demand for precision machined parts prompted the company to expand its facility in 1997 to 19,000 square feet, up from its original size of 7,500 square feet.

The Szabo's strong family commitment adds a sense of cohesiveness to the business. Members of the Szabo family serve as the company's officers, with Mike G. Szabo serving as president and his wife Tereza as treasurer. Sons, Mike and Denes, serve as operations managers, George as secretary, and daughter, Zsuzsanna is the office manager. The only non-family member, Tony Clarke, serves as sales director.

Along with Mile-Hi Machine's strong commitment to family, the company maintains a strong commitment to Jefferson County and Arvada in particular. Contributions are made to United Way, the Arvada Police Department, Fellowship of Christian Athletes and, most recently, the Arvada Center's Playground.

The quality service and commitment Mile-Hi Machine provides its clients has not gone unnoticed. Mile-Hi Machine, Inc. has been honored by Storage Tech, Micro Switch, Stanley Aviation and Hewlett Packard for its dedication and precision machining.

Above: Office located on West 56th Avenue in Arvada.

Below: Mile-Hi Machine, Inc. officers (from left) Mike I. Szabo, Tony Clarke, George Szabo, Denes Szabo, Mike G. Szabo, Tereza Szabo, and Zsuzsanna Moore.

COLORADO SCHOOL OF MINES

Above: Students come from all over the world, providing the school with a diverse blend of ideas and cultures.

Below: Tucked against the eastern slope of Lookout Mountain in Golden, Colorado School of Mines is the second oldest institution in the United States emphasizing minerals, materials science and energy engineering education.

Colorado School of Mines (CSM), tucked against the eastern slope of Lookout Mountain in Golden, is a public research university recognized for its leadership in engineering, applied science and related disciplines, with a special emphasis on the Earth and its resources.

Organized in 1869 and formally established under the Territory of Colorado in 1874, CSM was the first public institution of higher education to open its doors in the state. The university maintains its historic emphasis on the extractive industry engineering disciplines but has expanded into the fields of materials science, engineering, energy and the environment. Today, CSM offers a broad range of engineering disciplines and a full research program in engineering and applied science, with a particular focus on the responsible stewardship of the Earth's resources.

CSM has the largest enrollment and is the second oldest institution in the United States that emphasizes minerals, materials science and energy engineering education. Serving over 3,000 students annually, CSM is highly regarded internationally for its leadership in resource fields. Students and staff alike come from all over the world, providing the School with a diverse blend of ideas and cultures. Of the more than 200 full-time, tenured faculty members, more than 95 percent hold a Ph.D.

Maintaining high standards is key to CSM's success. Although course work is demanding, students have a variety of campus activities to choose from, including 16 varsity intercollegiate sports, the highest number available in any state-supported institution in Colorado. Nearly 20 percent of the student body participate in varsity sports and more than 50 percent are involved in intramurals.

CSM is a founding member of the Rocky Mountain Athletic Conference (RMAC), a member of NCAA Division II.

An integral part of the School's mission is outreach to the community, particularly to working professionals wishing to gain additional knowledge or upgrade their technical skills. CSM's Office of Special Programs and Continuing Education offers non-credit short courses, conferences, selected credit courses, certificate programs and recertification-credit classes for K-12 teachers.

Special facilities associated with CSM include: Arthur Lakes Library, which holds 340,000 monographs, 175,000 maps, 380,000 U.S. government publications and more than 2,000 active periodical titles; the Geology Museum, open to visitors year-round; the Edgar Mine, open for tours in Idaho Springs; Bunker Auditorium, Friedhoff Hall, Petroleum Hall, Metals Hall and the Ben Parker Student Center, all available for public events.

For more than 124 years, Colorado School of Mines' educational offerings have been among the best in the world. Recognized around the globe, its programs and graduates continue the School's tradition of excellence.

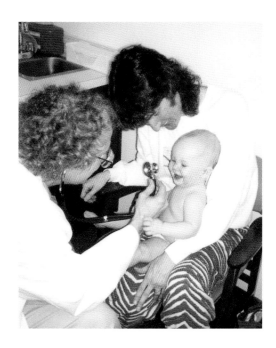

New West Physicians is a primary care group practice and medical management company consisting of sixty physicians and fifteen mid-level practitioners practicing at fifteen office locations throughout the Denver metro area. Within this group of professionals, thirty-five are in Family Practice and twenty-five in Internal Medicine. Combined, they serve 200,000 registered patients, 35,000 of whom participate in HMO health plans.

New West Physicians was incorporated in 1994. The organization is comprised of two companies—New West Physicians, P.C. which employs the physicians and New West Management Services, Inc. which performs the administrative and management services for the organization. Both companies are for-profit entities which are owned and governed by the participating physicians. To further service its clients, New West has established an independent physicians association (IPA) known as Health First IPA, which is a wholly owned subsidiary of the management services organization. Through the specialist IPA, New West has aligned itself with the most effective and talented specialists in the Denver metro area; those with top level skills in their specialized area of practice.

The twenty-three primary care physicians who first established New West were united by a vision of working together in a common structure with a shared purpose: to improve the physical, mental and spiritual health of the communities they serve and to provide an integrated, primary care-owned and managed healthcare delivery system that would allow them to remain competitive in the managed care marketplace.

Practice locations throughout the Denver metro area include Arvada, Aurora, Broomfield, Lakewood, Denver, Evergreen, Golden, Highlands Ranch and Thornton. At the present time, New West is actively recruiting additional practices in the Denver area and expects to reach 100 physicians by the year 2000.

New West serves all patient populations in the area. A strong patient focus and expertise in patient management has earned New West some of the region's most desirable HMO contracts. Under these contracts, the organization has the freedom to deliver the best care to its patients. To support its patients in their health plans, New West has created sophisticated practice management systems to relieve physicians of administrative burdens allowing them to focus more of their time and attention on patient care.

As a way to enhance the patients' experience with New West and in support of their future expansion, the organization is developing programs in disease management, patient education and patient communication and services. These programs will allow New West to remain the practice of choice for patients seeking healthcare services in the Denver metro area and specifically in Jefferson County.

Top: Dr. John Gale from the Golden Central Family Practice examines a new patient.

Below: Dr. Werner Baumgartner from Lakewood Internal Medicine meets with a patient.

FOOTHILLS CORPORATE LODGING

Above: Clean, comfortable surroundings to call home.

Below: The space and amenities to make living away from home relaxing.

Bottom: Tamarisk at the Lake in Littleton.

It's the little things that make a difference. And in the world of temporary housing, those little things can make the place you lay your head feel more like home.

Foothills Corporate Lodging, with its office located in Lakewood, provides fully furnished lodging alternatives for executives, families and their guests who are on special assignment in Denver, transferring to the area or between homes for any number of reasons. Options range from one- to three-bedroom apartment homes or townhomes, all within residential areas and in close proximity to shopping and quality restaurants. Length of stay can be as short as seven days or up to months in duration depending on housing needs.

Whether business travelers or families waiting for new homes to be built, residents are assured clean, up-to-date and well-maintained accommodations consisting of a completely furnished living room—most with a fireplace, dining room table and chairs, kitchen basics such as dishes, cookware, utensils, microwave, toaster and coffee maker, queen or twin beds, linens, pillows, dressers, table lamps, alarm clock, bath towels, tissue, soap, iron and ironing board, along with a washer and dryer in each unit. On some properties, extras such as movie channels, VCR, stereo, voice messaging, use of a pool and/or exercise room and an enclosed garage are also included. Weekly cleaning service is available, as are other amenities upon request.

Started in 1984, Foothills Corporate Lodging began by leasing one townhouse to Martin Marietta. Demand led to the acquisition of ten additional units within a short period of time. Today, Foothills operates 100 units sprinkled along the front range, most of which are located in Jefferson County. Calavera Apartments and Remington West in Westminster, The Heights in Lakewood, Jefferson at Raccoon Creek and Oasis Lakeway in Littleton, and Oasis Denver West in Golden are just a few of the Foothills locations many people have called home over the years.

A highly economical alternative to comparable accommodations (about one-half the cost of a first class hotel), real estate agents, insurance claims representatives and corporate placement departments have assisted clients and their own companies in saving money without sacrificing comfort, quality or convenience.

Foothills has a staff of nine employees to round out its office personnel, a full-time cleaning crew, a and full-time maintenance service.

As a family owned and operated business, Foothills Corporate Lodging is the leading full-time corporate lodging company in the west metro area dedicated to offering customized service to those needing a temporary home away from home.

The Butterfly Pavilion & Insect Center opened its doors in July 1995 to foster an appreciation of butterflies and other invertebrates and to educate the public about the need for conservation of threatened habitats around the world. Created by the Rocky Mountain Butterfly Consortium, a Colorado non-profit organization, the 16,000 square foot facility draws over 200,000 people each year to observe, discover, examine and delight in this zoological experience unique to Colorado. While there are nearly a dozen butterfly houses in the United States, Westminster's Butterfly Pavilion & Insect Center was the first stand alone non-profit insect zoo in the nation.

Visitors to the Pavilion, located on 104th Avenue and U.S. 36, will find themselves surrounded by more than 1,200 free-flying butterflies in the Wings of the Tropics conservatory. Many years of research went into creating the crucial climate controlled tropical environment that averages 80 degrees and 70% humidity even in the midst of winter. Over 100 species of tropical and subtropical plants are part of the habitat and were selected for their variety in color, size, shape, texture and food-producing nectar. In addition, a chrysalis viewing area allows visitors to watch the amazing process of metamorphosis as adult butterflies emerge from their gem-like chrysalides.

In the Crawl-a-see-ém, people of all ages can watch, touch or view close-up some of the world's most fascinating insects and their relatives. They can discover what it feels like to hold a rose-haired tarantula from Chile, a Madagascar Hissing Cockroach, or a giant mealworm. Easy-to-use microscopes allow visitors to zoom in on some startling insect specimens, such as spider legs and tarantula fangs.

At the Waters Edge exhibit, visitors have the opportunity to experience an up-close, hands-on look at the animals that live in the fragile habitat of both coastal shorelines including: sea stars, sea hares, peppermint shrimp, sea urchins, sea cucumbers, hermit crabs and other marine invertebrates.

To complement the Pavilion's inside exhibits, outdoor gardens have been planted to attract local butterflies. A cactus garden, herb garden, naturalized landscaping and a half-mile nature trail with interpretive signage surround the facility, all with highlights that vary with the seasons.

Educational offerings through the Butterfly Pavilion & Insect Center's Public Program series are available for participants of all ages. Children, families and adults can explore the marvels of nature through a variety of workshops and lectures focused on how plants and animals interrelate in the environment. While programs change seasonally, topics include family butterfly gardening, monarch migration, understanding backyard urban habitats and trekking the Amazon Rain Forest.

Above: The Common Morpho (Morpho peleides) (inset), one of more than fifty different butterfly species, makes its home in the Wings of the Tropics conservatory.
PHOTO COURTESY OF DON JARRETT.

Below: The Butterfly Pavilion is a place for people of all ages to observe, explore and delight in a unique zoological experience.
PHOTO COURTESY OF DAVID ENNIS.

CREDIT UNION OF THE ROCKIES

Credit Union of the Rockies is a member-owned financial cooperative dedicated to providing low-cost, high quality consumer financial services for members. Headquartered in Golden, and with offices in the Denver West Business Park and Frisco, the credit union serves 7,500 people in Jefferson, Clear Creek and Summit Counties.

Chartered by the State of Colorado in 1937 for employees of the USDA, Credit Union of the Rockies has grown to a $30 million organization which also serves the financial needs of 300 local businesses' employees and their families.

As a member of the Credit Union Service Centers network, members can find convenient access to their credit union accounts at more than twenty locations in Colorado and at more than 250 service centers nationwide.

Credit Union of the Rockies is directed by a seven member volunteer Board of Directors elected by their fellow members. Their dedication of time, talent and energy over the years has enabled Credit Union of the Rockies to achieve the success it celebrated in 1998 with its 60th anniversary and the opening of the credit union's new office at 607 Nineteenth Street in Golden.

Well-known in the community for its involvement in the Greater Golden Chamber of Commerce and Downtown Golden Merchants Association, the credit union was also recognized in 1998 as an award-winning participant in the American Cancer Society Relay for Life. The credit union sponsors Little League Baseball and is involved in numerous other community activities.

Margie Knodel, President/CEO, has made it her mission to be an active leader in the credit union community. She serves as Vice Chairman of the Board of Directors for the Colorado Credit Union League, the trade association for the state's 186 credit unions. Knodel has worked diligently in helping to lead a grassroots effort to ensure that consumers have the right to choose their financial institutions. A result of this commitment was the recent passage of the Credit Union Membership Access Act by the United States Congress.

With more than twenty years experience in the industry, Knodel is an advocate for providing consumers the choice to use a credit union—a place where members find financially sound, customized services to meet their specific financial needs, with savings federally insured to $100,000 per member by the National Credit Union Administration.

Involvement, dedication and personal interest make Credit Union of the Rockies a highly valued, locally member-owned financial cooperative in Jefferson County. It has much to be proud of, as do its member-owners.

Above: Credit Union of the Rockies' new corporate center, located at 607 Nineteenth Street, Golden, accommodates members' needs through service center and electronic access. The facility was designed to propel Credit Union of the Rockies into the next millennium.

Below: David Wheeler, Chairman of the Board, and Margie Knodel, President/CEO, celebrate Credit Union of the Rockies' 60th anniversary and grand opening of the new Golden facility with a ribbon cutting ceremony.

PHOTOS COURTESY OF COLORADO CREDIT UNION LEAGUE

PHOTO CREDITS

REFERENCES

From Scratch: A History of
Jefferson County, Colorado
by Members of the Jefferson County
Historical Commission

History of Pioneer Wheat Ridge
Historical Committee,
Wheat Ridge, Colorado

History of Jefferson County, Colorado
Ethel Dark

Waters of Gold
Arvada Historical Society

Mount Vernon Country Clubhouse,
Then & Now
Georgia Brown
The Arvada Enterprise

Colorado Trivia
J. Murphey Lenahan
Ruthledge Hill Press

The Colorado Quick-Fact Book
Midwest Research Institute
Capper Press

Denver Metro Economic Profile 1997
Metro Denver Network

A Colorado History
Ubbelohde, Benson, Smith
6th Edition, Pruett Publishing

Jefferson County Colorado:
Colorful Past of a Great Community
Sara E. Robbins
Published by The Jefferson
County Bank

Birds of Colorado
Alfred M. Bailey and Robert Niedrach
Denver Museum of Natural History

American Indians in Colorado
J. Donald Hughes
Pruett Publishing

The Story of The Homestead Act
R. Conrad Slein
Childrens Press

People of the Red Earth
Sally Crum
Ancient City Press

Colorado, Visions of an American Landscape
Kenneth I Helphand, Roberts Rinehart,
Publishers

The Making of Arva-Pride
William Cheesman
Arvada Historical Society

Biographical Sketches: Early Settlers
of Wheat Ridge
Wheat Ridge Historical Committee

History of Pioneer Wheat Ridge
Historical Committee
Wheat Ridge, Colorado

Arvada United Methodist Church 1870-1970
Ted Johnson

Lakewood Colorado, An Illustrated Biography
Patricia K (Pat) Wilcox
Lakewood 25th Birthday Commission

INDEX